Geoffrey Landesman

ON BORROWED TIME

Based on the novel of the same name by
Lawrence Edward Watkin

ACTING EDITION

★

COMEDY IN TWO ACTS

BY PAUL OSBORN

★

DRAMATISTS
PLAY SERVICE
INC.

ACKNOWLEDGMENT

The author and publisher wish to thank Mr. K. Elmo Lowe, Associate Director of the Cleveland Play House, for permission to use in the present edition his prompt script of this play, as produced by him at the Play House. Mr. Lowe's version not only makes it possible to produce the play in one simple set but also eliminates several curtains and all waits between scenes; thus giving the play flow and tempo that are essential to a tight production.

The accompanying diagrams, on pages 70 and 71, executed by Sol Cornberg, Technical Director, and Gulielma Daves, Scene Designer, are furnished with the photograph of the set through the courtesy of the Play House.

The original edition of ON BORROWED TIME, with text conforming to the New York production, is published in cloth covers by Alfred A. Knopf, Inc.

ON BORROWED TIME was originally produced by Dwight Deere Wiman, at the Longacre Theater, New York, February 3, 1938. It was directed by Joshua Logan, and the settings were by Jo Mielziner.

Following is the program of the revised acting edition of the play as printed in the present book, as produced at the Play House, Cleveland, Charles S. Brooks Theatre, and staged by K. Elmo Lowe with the following cast:

PUD	Joel David Katz
JULIAN NORTHRUP, Gramps	Dudley Digges
NELLIE, Granny	Helen Watkins
MR. BRINK	Harvey Miller
MARCIA GILES	Evelyn Chevillat
DEMETRIA RIFFLE	Esther Mullin
A BOY	Neil Hollander
WORKMEN	Nathan Heller, Mark Hipkins
DR. EVANS	Kirk Willis
MR. PILBEAM	Thomas R. Ireland
MR. GRIMES	Julian Benjamin
SHERIFF	Stanley Anderson
BETTY	Flora McDonald

The entire action takes place in the living room and the back yard of the Northrup home.

ACT I

SCENE 1. Afternoon.

SCENE 2. A week later.

SCENE 3. Dusk, a week later.

INTERMISSION

ACT II

SCENE 1. Two hours later.

SCENE 2. Ten o'clock that night.

SCENE 3. Dawn, the next morning.

SCENE 4. Dusk, the same day.

SCENE 5. A few minutes later, the same day.

SCENE 6. Later that night.

Direction Assistance, Gordon Hatfield; Setting designd and executed by Sol Cornberg and Guliema Daves; Stage Manager, Ben Letter.

Play House direction, Frederic McConnell; Associate direction, K. Elmo Lowe; Assistant direction, Max Eisenstat; Technical direction, Sol Cornberg; Public Relations, Hildegarde Darmstadter.

ON BORROWED TIME

ACT I

For arrangement of the setting, see diagram on page 71.
NOTE: *Lights. The whole stage is always lighted, exterior as exterior—interior as interior. The playing areas are always the hottest but without any attempt to blot out the section of stage that is not in use. Three very small baby spots should be used inside the room itself so that the room can be hot and the fore stage or exterior moonlight.*

SCENE 1: *Late afternoon.*

AT RISE: GRAMPS *seated chair* R. *of table, engraving fob.* PUD *looks out door* R.

PUD. (*Crosses to above table,* L. *of* GRAMPS.) You could write Pud on it afterwards.

GRAMPS. Yeh! I could write shikepoke on it too, but I ain't goin' to.

PUD. What's shikepoke?

GRAMPS. A shikepoke's a bird.

PUD. Is it what you call the bird?

GRAMPS. Yup. (*Pause.*)

PUD. If the watch fob belonged to the bird would you write shikepoke on it?

GRAMPS. Birds don't have watch fobs.

PUD. But if it did have one would you write shikepoke on it, Gramps?

GRAMPS. Expect I would.

PUD. Because it's what you call the bird, isn't it, Gramps? (PUD *crosses* L. C. *Sits chair* L.)

GRAMPS. That's right, sonny. (GRAMPS *is busy.*)

PUD. Gramps, what do you call me?

GRAMPS. Eh? Oh, I call you all sorts of things — sonny, chummy ——

PUD. No, no! What's the *name* you call me?
GRAMPS. Oh, Pud, you mean. Pud. That's what you look like. Pud.
PUD. It's what you call me, isn't it, Gramps?
GRAMPS. That's right, sonny.
PUD. Then if the watch fob belongs to me and you call me Pud you ought to write Pud on it. If the shikepoke had a fob ——
GRAMPS. Whoa there! I said I wasn't gonna write Pud on this here fob!
PUD. But Pud's my name.
GRAMPS. Your name is John Gilford Northrup. And that's what I'm gonna engrave on this here fob. John Gilford Northrup.
PUD. I like Pud better.
GRAMPS. Pud's too easy, P-U-D. John Gilford Northrup. And don't you forget it. (PUD *crosses* L. *to sideboard. Pause.* GRAMPS *works.* PUD *crosses* L. *to desk.*)
PUD. Where's Mom gone today, Gramps?
GRAMPS. She's gone with your father.
PUD. Where did he go?
GRAMPS. Up to Gainesville to make a call.
PUD. (*Works up* L. C.) Is somebody sick?
GRAMPS. Somebody's always sick, sonny. (*Pause.*)
PUD. I'm going to be a doctor when I grow up, too.
GRAMPS. You bet you are. You're gonna be as good a doctor as your daddy.
PUD. Maybe better. (PUD *crosses to* L. *of* GRAMPS.)
GRAMPS. That's a stiff order, sonny. Your daddy's a A number one doctor.
PUD. What's A number one? (*Pause.* PUD *puts* GRAMPS' *arm around him.*) What's A number one, Gramps?
GRAMPS. Oh, it's just A number one. There. Now, what do you think of that? (PUD *looks at fob.*)
PUD. I guess it's all right, Gramps.
GRAMPS. What do you mean you guess it's all right?
PUD. (*Leans on arm of chair.*) Well, that G looks a little more like a C, I think.
GRAMPS. You do? Let's see. (*Takes fob.*)
PUD. My name is John Gilford Northrup. Not John Cilford Northrup ——
GRAMPS. I know that, boy, I know that. Well, guess that G does

need a little more of a tail there. Yes, sir, I guess it does. Thank you, boy.

PUD. You're welcome, Gramps. (PUD *crosses up* L. C. *to shelf with stones.*) Guess we better take a walk out to Milbaur Park one of these days, Gramps. We need some more stones for our collection.

GRAMPS. (*Reaching in pocket.*) Oh, here's a bone I found yesterday down by the meatshop. (PUD *crosses* C. *to above table.*)

PUD. Is it a human bone, Gramps?

GRAMPS. (*Gives bone to* PUD.) Might be——

PUD. Looks pretty human to me, Gramps.

GRAMPS. Might be.

PUD. It's a very fine specimen, anyway, Gramps. (PUD *takes bone, crosses* U. L. C. *to shelf. Gets frog, crosses* C. *to* GRAMPS *again.*) This frog's gettin' kinda old, Gramps.

GRAMPS. Yep. Guess we'll have to throw that old frog out in a few days.

PUD. It's a very fine specimen though, Gramps. (PUD *crosses* U. L. C. *to shelf with frog. Holds.*)

GRAMPS. We'll get another one.

PUD. (*Suddenly. Singing.*)
Aunt Demetria is a pismire.
Aunt Demetria is a pismire.

GRAMPS. Hey, there. Where did you hear that?

PUD. You told Granny she was.

GRAMPS. You mustn't use that word about your Aunt Demetria.

PUD. (PUD *crosses* C. *above table to* GRAMPS.) *You* said she was a pismire.

GRAMPS. She *is* a pismire! She's the biggest pismire I know. You know what a pismire is, sonny?

PUD. No.

GRAMPS. It's an ant, and it's one of the meanest of ants that crawls. And your Aunt Demetria is a pismire. But you mustn't say it. It makes your Granny mad.

PUD. But why is Aunt Demetria so mean, Gramps? (PUD *crosses* R. *to below* GRAMPS. *Climbs on his knee.*)

GRAMPS. Born that way.

PUD. Why was she born that way?

GRAMPS. I'll tell you, boy, it's like this. Your other Gramps——

PUD. What Gramps?

GRAMPS. I say when your other Gramps was alive . . .

PUD. What other Gramps?

GRAMPS. Your Mom's father. Pshaw, boy, didn't you know you used to have another Gramps? Everybody has two Gramps.

PUD. (*Tearfully.*) But I don't want any other Gramps, Gramps. Did you have another Pud?

GRAMPS. No, 'course I didn't, boy. You're the only Pud I ever had.

PUD. (*Hits table.*) Then you're the only Gramps I ever had.

GRAMPS. All right, boy, all right. That other fellow—we'll call him your grandfather. Is that all right?

PUD. I guess so, Gramps.

GRAMPS. All right, then. So your grandfather had a whole lot of children. And the first one he had was your Aunt Demetria. That was a long time ago, when your grandfather was a young buck and didn't have no sense at all, so he didn't do a very good job of it. Botched it up all the way round. Then he had a lot more children to practice on and the last one he had was your mother. Now, there he did a real sweet job. Yes, sir, a pretty nigh perfect job. (PUD *off knee to* D. R.)

PUD. But he sure made a mess out of Aunt Demetria.

GRAMPS. That's what I've been trying to tell you, boy.

GRANNY. (*Off-stage.*) Juleyun!

GRAMPS. Oh, hell! (GRAMPS *takes bottle from pocket.*)

PUD. Where is hell, Gramps?

GRAMPS. Where the woodbine twineth. (*Takes sip from bottle.*) Don't you ever touch this, boy.

PUD. Give me some. (PUD *close to* GRAMPS.)

GRAMPS. No ——

PUD. Just a little taste. . . .

GRAMPS. You wouldn't like 'er, boy!

PUD. Please, Gramps, please.

GRAMPS. Here then, teach yourself. (PUD *takes bottle. Bus.* D. R. *As* PUD *takes drink* GRANNY *calls again.* PUD *spits it out.*)

GRANNY. (*Off-stage.*) Juleyun!

PUD. (*Wipes mouth.*) Peeyew!

GRAMPS. Well, I warned you. (GRAMPS *takes bottle.*)

PUD. What do you drink it for, Gramps?

GRAMPS. I drink it for my ches . . . because I li . . . oh, because your Granny is yellin' at me and I got to take that damn smelly dog out for a walk. (PUD *leans over* GRAMPS.)

PUD. But I like the way Betty smells.

GRAMPS. You're welcome to it. (GRANNY *on* U. *from* L. *arch. Crosses to* C. *above table.* GRAMPS *hides bottle as* GRANNY *comes in with dog.*)

GRANNY. (*Crosses to table.*) When you two get together over some gimcrack you're as deaf as a post. (PUD *holds* R. C.)

GRAMPS. Was you calling, Miss Nellie? Didn't hear you.

GRANNY. (*Crosses* R. C.) None so deaf as those who don't want to hear.

GRAMPS. Well, what d'ye want?

GRANNY. I hollered loud enough to wake the dead. Go with your Grandpa, Betty.

GRAMPS. (*Takes leash.*) And I'll thank you not to claim kin to me with that bitch!

GRANNY. Julian! (*Points to* PUD.)

GRAMPS. Pshaw, that's what she is . . . no more, no less than a bitch.

PUD. (*Singing, suddenly. Dances* R. C.) A dog or a bitch, you never know which. (*Both look at* PUD.)

GRANNY. There you are!

GRAMPS. I never taught him that, Miss Nellie, I swear.

GRANNY. Turning your own grandson into a smutty mouth like yourself.

GRAMPS. Honest, I never taught him that, Miss Nellie.

GRANNY. That I should live to see the day . . . ! (GRANNY *rises and crosses* U. C.)

GRAMPS. Oh, come along, Petunia.

GRANNY. (*Leaning toward* GRAMPS.) And her name isn't Petunia.

GRAMPS. All right, come along, Sweet Pea.

PUD. (*Up* R. *to* GRAMPS.) I'll take her, Gramps. (PUD *crosses* U. C., *takes leash.*) It's kinda *hot* for you to be out today.

GRAMPS. I guess you're right. It is. Thank you kindly. Go with your uncle, Betty.

PUD. Am I her uncle?

GRAMPS. (*Looking toward* GRANNY.) Seems so. (GRAMPS *crosses* D. R. *Sits chair* R. *Holds* L. C. *above table.*)

GRANNY. He mimics everything you do. He hardly has a chance to see his own father. Jim's always so busy. First thing you know, that boy'll grow up and be just like you. Is that what you want?

GRAMPS. Nope. I want him to go further'n I have.

GRANNY. Then you better set him an example. You gotta stop

swearin' and smokin' that smelly pipe. You never draw a breath that it ain't full of smokin' and swearin'. You better change your ways, Julian Northrup. If you don't, I'm gonna talk to Jim and Susan about sending Pud away to school.

GRAMPS. Send him away to school? At his age?

GRANNY. It'd be better for him than being around you so much.

GRAMPS. There ain't no school what'd take him. He's too little.

GRANNY. Yes, there is. Demetria knows a school in . . .

GRAMPS. Demetria! By God, I might have known she was at the bottom of this. (GRANNY *looks at him.*) Old bird-stuffer!

GRANNY. Demetria's a fine, Christian woman and I won't hear a word against her.

GRAMPS. She's a bird-stuffer!

GRANNY. She's no such thing.

GRAMPS. Oh, Miss Nellie—I don't see why you're always sticking up for Demmie. She's a bird-stuffer and you know it.

GRANNY. Demmie may have her faults but she's a God-fearing woman. She's warned Susan time and time again how you're poisoning Pud's mind, and now she's found this nice boarding-school run by a Baptist woman.

GRAMPS. Baptist woman! By gosh, Pud's not goin' to no school run by a Baptist woman.

GRANNY. Then you better change your ways, Julian Northrup. (*Crosses to her.*) You are a bad influence on the boy and it's gotta be stopped. It's gotta be. (*He pats her. She crosses* R. *to door. Pause. She looks at* GRAMPS.) What is a bird-stuffer, Julian?

GRAMPS. It's just a bird-stuffer.

GRANNY. But it must *mean* something.

GRAMPS. Nope. It don't. Adam saw a dog and it looked like a dog and he called it a dog. I saw Demmie, she looked like a bird-stuffer and I called her a bird-stuffer, so she is a bird-stuffer. (*Pause.*)

GRANNY. Sultry today, ain't it?

GRAMPS. Hotter'n a bull mink in matin' season.

GRANNY. That I don't know about. (GRAMPS *laughs. Pause.*) Guess we'll have another shower. Hope it won't spoil Susan's day. She so seldom goes with Jim on a case.

GRAMPS. (*Crossing to window.*) What did she go for today?

GRANNY. For the pleasure of bein' with him.

GRAMPS. (*Singing.*)

She remained up in the mountains,
She remained up in the mountains,
(*He crosses* U. C.)
Remained up in the mountains all that night.

GRANNY. Julian. I just don't feel very well. I think I'll go upstairs now. (*She goes out. He off to* L. *arch.*)

GRAMPS. (*Back of chair* R. *of table.*) All right, Miss Nellie. I'll come and lie down, too, soon as Pud comes in. I'm feelin' kind of tired myself. (*Crosses* U. R. *to shelves* R. *of arch. Sings.*)
Her life is beer and skittles
And she is eating fancy vittles
And them West Virginia . . .
(*Crosses down* R., *has spasm.* BRINK *appears* U. C. *and from off* R. *Holds.* GRAMPS *sits chair* R., *bows head—then* BRINK *speaks.*)

BRINK. Mr. Julian Northrup, I believe?

GRAMPS. What's that? I didn't catch it.

BRINK. Most people don't hear me the first time. (GRAMPS *holds chair* R. BRINK *holds door.*)

GRAMPS. How in blazes could I hear you if I was asleep?

BRINK. Are you sure you were—asleep?

GRAMPS. Guess I musta drowsed off. Felt kind of tired all of a sudden. Who are you? What d'ye want?

BRINK. I request that you come with me.

GRAMPS. Where yuh goin'?

BRINK. Where the woodbine twineth.

GRAMPS. Where the wood . . . ? *I* just said that. I made it up. It's what yuh say to a child. *I* ain't no child.

BRINK. Aren't you?

GRAMPS. No, I'm not. Say, look here, who the hell are you?

BRINK. You may call me Mr. Brink.

GRAMPS. Well, look here, Mr. Brink, I don't like you. I wouldn't go with you to a rat fight, so now you know.

BRINK. I'm sorry.

GRAMPS. I don't like the way you snuck up here. I don't like the way you talk.

BRINK. I'm afraid that will have to be as it may be.

GRAMPS. Oh, you are! (*Rises, has spasm, sits again.*) Well, you better . . . (*Rises.*) get out of here right awa . . .

BRINK. You see. It's time for you to come with me. (GRAMPS *never looks direct at* BRINK.)

GRAMPS. No . . . no . . . It ain't. I ain't goin' nowhere. I'm goin' to stay right here. I'm waitin' for Pud. You get the hell out of here! (*Rises, crosses* R. C.) You git off my son's property! You git the . . . (BRINK *off* U. C. *to* R. *before* GRANNY *turns up.*)

GRANNY. (*Off-stage.*) Julian!

GRAMPS. You git the . . . (*Discovers* BRINK *has disappeared, is bewildered.*) Well, I'll be . . . (GRAMPS *sits chair* R. GRANNY *on* U. *from* L. *of arch, crosses down to table.*)

GRANNY. Who you shoutin' at that way?

GRAMPS. Well, I . . . there was a feller here. . . .

GRANNY. Well, where is he?

GRAMPS. He's gone now.

GRANNY. What did he want?

GRAMPS. I don't rightly know, Miss Nellie. I . . .

GRANNY. You better come upstairs out of that hot room, Julian. (*Goes off* U. *to* L. *of arch.*)

GRAMPS. Yes, I guess I better had. (PUD *on* U. *from* R. *of arch. Crosses to above table. To* GRAMPS.)

PUD. Gramps, who was that man?

GRAMPS. You seen him, did you, son?

PUD. Sure. He was coming down the walk. Who was he?

GRAMPS. I don't rightly know who he was.

PUD. What did he want?

GRAMPS. He wanted me to go with him.

PUD. Where?

GRAMPS. Where the woodbine twineth.

PUD. Oh! You mean, Hell.

GRAMPS. By golly, boy, we better both go upstairs out of this hot room. (GRAMPS *and* PUD *cross* U. C. *Hold in arch. Surveys room.* GRAMPS *grunts.*)

CURTAIN

ACT I

SCENE 2: *Late afternoon. A week later.*

AT RISE: PUD *is reading on floor.* GRAMPS *is writing.* GRANNY, *seated in chair* L. *of table, is knitting.*

GRANNY. (MARCIA *on down* L. *crosses* U. C. *above table, with glass. Gives* GRANNY *drink.*) Thank you, Marcy. I'll just keep it here till I need it. (*Wipes eyes with mourning handkerchief.*)
MARCIA. How are you feeling, Mrs. Northrup?
GRANNY. Won't be long before I'm flat on my back for good, now.
MARCIA. (*Patting* GRANNY'S *shoulder.* MARCIA *crosses* U. R. *to desk, opens it, gets ink. Crosses* C. *to table with ink. Holds.*) Oh, you got years and years yet, Mrs. Northrup.
GRANNY. Don't know as I want years and years yet.
GRAMPS. Anyways, where the hell's some more ink?
MARCIA. Here's some, Mr. Northrup.
GRAMPS. Oh, thank ye, Marcy. How did we ever find things before you came to live with us? (MARCIA *crosses* U. R. *Puts ink in desk, leaves it open. Pause.* GRAMPS *writes.* GRANNY *knits.*)
PUD. (*Suddenly.*) Granny, why do they put dead peoples in coffings?
GRANNY. Oh, Pud! (*She crosses* L. C. *to above* GRAMPS. *Buries her face in her hands, crying suddenly.*)
GRAMPS. There, there, Miss Nellie! (*Rises, crosses to her.*) Now, don't talk about that any more, boy.
PUD. But why do they, Gramps? (MARCIA *crosses* D. R. *to* PUD, *stoops.*)
MARCIA. 'Cause that's the way you take care of 'em. Now, read your story, Pud. (MARCIA *crosses* U. R. *Closes desk, then off* U. C. *to* L. *arch.* PUD *is quiet.*)
GRAMPS. That's all right, Miss Nellie. That's all right.
GRANNY. (*Looking up at him.*) I don't know—I'm just so tired, Julian.
GRAMPS. 'Course you are. Now, everything's all right, Miss Nellie. (*Kisses her on forehead, crosses to chair* R. *Sits.*)

PUD. Is it comfable in a coffing?

GRAMPS. Yes, boy, very comfortable in a coffin.

PUD. As comfortable as my bed?

GRAMPS. Sure, sure. 'Course it is. As comfortable as your bed. (*Motioning to book on floor.*) Now read your damn story. (*Pause.* GRANNY *gets hold of herself.*)

GRANNY. It's very comfortable in a coffin, Pud.

PUD. (*Suddenly. Rises.*) My mamma and papa are in coffings. They put them in the ground like this —— (*Kneels. Illustrates.*) You may lower now. Dear Lord, we commend to thy tender ——

GRAMPS. (*Turning quickly.*) Don't, Pud. Don't. I told you ——

GRANNY. That's all right, Julian. (PUD *crosses to* L. *of* GRANNY. *She takes him in her arms.*) Yes, dear, your mamma and papa are both very comfortable.

PUD. My papa was a brave man, wasn't he?

GRANNY. Yes, he was, dear—very brave.

PUD. He turned his automobile right off the road so he wouldn't hurt a little boy just like me.

GRANNY. That's right, darling.

PUD. (*As though repeating a lesson.*) But I must never forget that my dear mamma and papa were taken from me and I will never, never have any others. I'm a—orphan.

GRAMPS. (*Quickly.*) Who told you that?

PUD. Aunt Demetria. (PUD *crosses* R. C. *to book on floor.*)

GRAMPS. (*Roaring, pointing to* GRANNY.) There! That damned old ——!

GRANNY. Julian!

GRAMPS. Telling things like that to the boy! If that damned old hellion ——

GRANNY. Julian! If you swear any more like that in front of ——

GRAMPS. It's enough to make a preacher swear.

PUD. I'm going to swear when I'm nine.

GRAMPS. (*Shaking his finger.*) Ah—ah ——

PUD. (*Crossing to* GRAMPS.) But you said I could, Gramps. (GRAMPS *motions violently for* PUD *to go back to his book.* PUD *sits.* GRAMPS *ad lib., "Well, I guess that'll do." Refers to letter he's writing.*)

GRANNY. (*Angrily.*) There! Did you tell that boy he could . . . Did you tell that boy he could . . . (PUD *down on floor again.*

Looks at book. GRANNY *drinks.* GRAMPS *writes. Pause.*) Who you writin' to, anyway, Julian?

GRAMPS. Reverend Murdock. Looked pretty shabby when he was preachin' that funeral sermon. I guess preachin' don't pay what it used to. (*Pause.* GRAMPS *writes.*)

GRANNY. What are you writin' him for?

GRAMPS. Goin' to send him a check for $50.00. (*Turning to* GRANNY.) Now, that's a good deed, ain't it, even if I do say so myself?

GRANNY. Good deeds and leadin' a Christian life is two different things.

PUD. (*Rising to his knees, excited.*) Oh, Gramps, if you do a good deed, you can make a wish and it'll come true.

GRAMPS. (*Back at desk.*) What's that?

PUD. If you do a good deed, you can make a wish and it'll come true.

GRAMPS. That so, boy?

PUD. That's what my book says.

GRAMPS. Must be so then.

PUD. (*Very excited.*) So make a wish, Gramps, make a wish, make a wish.

GRAMPS. All right, boy, soon's I think of a good one. (*Pause. Turns to* GRANNY.) Listen, Miss Nellie, how does this sound? "Dear Reverend Murdock: Enclosed is a check for $50.00, for which please kindly send me one copy of the sermon you preached at the funeral of my son, James Northrup, M. D., and his wife, Susan. If you don't have it down on paper, maybe you wouldn't mind writing out the gist of the thing which I thought was very good and proper and appropriate to the occasion. I hope the enclosed check will compensate in some part for the trouble this will make you. Yours truly, Julian Northrup." Now, you don't think he'd take offense at that, do you?

GRANNY. I don't think so, Julian.

GRAMPS. (*Turning back to desk.*) No. Don't want to offend the old bastard.

GRANNY. (*Rising.*) Julian!

GRAMPS. Sorry, Miss Nellie. Take it back. Forgot. (PUD *rises* D. C. *Pause.*)

PUD. I'm going to the twalet.

GRANNY. What!

PUD. I'm going to the twalet.

GRANNY. Well, you don't have to tell the neighbors about it. When you have to go, just get up quietly and go. (PUD *crosses* U. L. *off* U. *to* L. *arch.*)

GRAMPS. Just say you have to wash your hands, boy. (GRANNY *and* GRAMPS *hold table.*)

GRANNY. Go along, Pud! (PUD *runs upstairs.* GRANNY *puts up knitting. Does not use again till* DEMETRIA *gives it to her.*) 'Twasn't an accident!

GRAMPS. What's that?

GRANNY. 'Twasn't an accident that killed Jim and Susan.

GRAMPS. Sure, of course it was, Miss Nellie—they turned over in their car.

GRANNY. God took Jim and Susan, Julian.

GRAMPS. Oh. Oh! (*Goes back to writing.*)

GRANNY. As a warnin' to us. Julian, I heard the voice of God at the funeral. I was sittin' there durin' the hymn, askin' myself why this cross had been put upon us. What had we done that was bad? And suddenly it came to me. It was you!

GRAMPS. Me?

GRANNY. You and me both, Julian.

GRAMPS. Well, what've we been doin' that's bad, Miss Nellie? I can't think of nothin'. Less you been up to somethin'.

GRANNY. I have, Julian. I've been closing my eyes to the way you've been ruinin' Pud. We can't raise a little boy, Julian—all by ourselves—we're too old.

GRAMPS. Why, sure we can, Miss Nellie—same way we raised Jim. I'll keep teaching him to cuss and you'll keep teaching him not to. He'll turn out pretty good, you'll see.

GRANNY. (*Turning away.*) We gotta find some other way to raise that boy.

GRAMPS. Ain't nobody goin' to raise that boy but us!

GRANNY. (*Turning to him.*) Julian, the Lord said . . .

GRAMPS. The Lord be blowed —— You heard the voice of Demetria.

GRANNY. No, it 'twasn't. It was the Lord's!

GRAMPS. It was Demetria's!

GRANNY. Julian Northrup, I guess I know the difference between the Lord's voice and Demetria Riffle's. (PUD *enters from* L. *of arch. Crosses* R. C. *to* GRAMPS.)

PUD. (*Pointing to his pants.*) Back door's undone.

GRAMPS. (*Pushes him.*) Go to your Granny. (PUD *backs to* GRANNY.)

GRANNY. Yes, come here, darling. I'll help you. (GRANNY *fastens pants.*) Get you all buttoned up nice and tight. (*Tries to kiss him.*) Got a nice kiss for Granny? (PUD *pulls up* C.) What's the matter, darling?

PUD. I've had too much ladies' arms around me lately.

GRANNY. Too *many* arms.

PUD. Too many arms. I'd like to have none arms around me for a while.

GRANNY. Oh, very well.

GRAMPS. You hadn't ought to say things like that to your Granny. If she wants to give you a kiss now and then, just let her do it.

PUD. She kisses awful wet.

GRAMPS. What the —— That don't cut no ice. . . . (BOY *on* R. *above tree. Climbs.*) And I don't want to ever see you smoke or say dirty things . . . and, above all . . . (PUD *crosses* R. C. *to door.* BOY *shakes finger at* PUD.) I don't ever want to hear you swear. . . . (*Turns, looks triumphantly at* GRANNY. PUD, *at this point, has turned and is staring out of door* R.)

PUD. Gramps, Gramps, somebody's stealing the apples again.

GRAMPS. Damn it to hell. (GRAMPS *rises. Crosses* R. *to door.* PUD *below him.*) Where is he?

PUD. He's up the tree.

GRAMPS. (*Shouting out door.*) Hey, you damn young shikepoke. (BOY *climbs over* D. *side of tree.*) I'm comin' out there and get you. You wait right there.

PUD. Hurry, Gramps, he's coming down.

GRAMPS. You stay up there. I'm goin' to give you such a tannin' ——

PUD. He's gettin' away, Gramps.

GRAMPS. (*Crossing closer to window.*) Hey, there—wait. . . . (BOY *drops from tree, exits* D. R.)

PUD. (*Turning around from window.*) Oh, Gramps, he got away. He didn't wait.

GRAMPS. (*Snapping fingers.*) Oh, hell —— (GRAMPS *and* PUD *cross* R. C.)

GRANNY. (*Laughs.*) Heh! Heh!

GRAMPS. I swear I wish that anyone who climbed that tree would have to stay up there until I let him down.

PUD. Gramps, you made a wish!

GRAMPS. Huh?

PUD. A wish! You wished anyone who climbed that tree would have to stay there until you let him down.

GRAMPS. (GRAMPS *crosses* U. R.) A lot of good it'll do me.

PUD. (*Jumps around excitedly.* PUD *crosses to* GRAMPS *above table.*) Gee, I bet we catch one of those bad boys up there and we can keep him up there for a hundred years. Maybe for a million years. Maybe. (DEMETRIA *on from* R. *arch* U. C. PUD *stops suddenly and becomes very quiet, staring at door.* DEMETRIA *enters, takes off hat, puts it on hat-rack.*)

GRANNY. (*Following* PUD'S *eyes.*) Oh, hello, Demmie.

GRAMPS. Oh, hell.

GRANNY. Come right in. (DEMETRIA *crosses* L. C. *to* PUD *above table.*)

DEMETRIA. Poor little lambie, what's the matter? Is he still thinking of his mamma and papa?

GRAMPS. Leave that boy alone, for God's sake!

GRANNY. Julian!

DEMETRIA. Well!

PUD. (*Struggling.*) Let me go!

DEMETRIA. There, there, lambie, your Aunt Demetria understands. (*Ruffles* PUD'S *hair. He straightens it with a defiant gesture.*) You must be a brave boy, boy. God has taken . . .

GRAMPS. Leave that boy alone, I say. (GRAMPS *crosses* R. C. PUD *crosses* R. C. *to* GRAMPS, *below table.*)

DEMETRIA. Would you deny the child Christian comfort, his parents hardly cold in their graves . . . ?

GRAMPS. (*Clasping* PUD.) To hell with Christian comfort, you old . . .

DEMETRIA. Come here, Pud.

PUD. I hate you!

GRAMPS. Now you know.

DEMETRIA. Come here to me, Pud.

GRAMPS. Like hell he will!

PUD. Like hell I will!

DEMETRIA. (*To* GRANNY.) See! See! (*To* GRAMPS.) You whited sepulchre!

GRAMPS. What! Whited sepulch . . . You—*woman* of Babylon! You ——

PUD. You—pismire!

GRAMPS. (*Taking his hand.*) That's right, boy. Come along. (GRAMPS *and* PUD *cross* R. *out door and off* R. *above tree.*) Let's get out of this company. (DEMETRIA *gives* R. C.)

DEMETRIA. You heard it, Nellie.

GRANNY. I never thought I'd live to ——

DEMETRIA. You heard what he called me! He called me . . . (DEMETRIA *to* R. *of table.*)

GRANNY. I know. Revelations 17:5. Don't say it, Demmie.

DEMETRIA. Of course, (DEMETRIA *sits chair* R.) I know I'm a nobody, Nellie. Maybe I'm no better than some folks say I am. But I'm certainly not a ——

GRANNY. Of course you're not, Demmie. I don't know what Julian was thinking of.

DEMETRIA. And he said it right in front of that sweet little boy. But, then, of course, it's none of my business.

GRANNY. Of course it's your business.

DEMETRIA. No. I guess I better stay home after this. I'm a downright nuisance.

GRANNY. You're not. You're a dear, sweet, Christian woman and you shouldn't always be runnin' yourself down. You're the only God-fearing woman . . . Well! . . . Maybe that's what the voice of God meant.

DEMETRIA. What?

GRANNY. I wonder if you shouldn't bring Pud up?

DEMETRIA. Me?

GRANNY. Your own sister's child. And you could bring him up the way God wants him to be brought up. Maybe that's what God meant.

DEMETRIA. Well, Nellie, I've thought about it. (DEMETRIA *to chair* R. GRANNY *chair* L.) But I couldn't afford to give Pud all the things he's been used to. That is, unless Jim left a will—or something like that.

GRANNY. Well, he did, Demmie. He left a will.

DEMETRIA. (*Sits.*) Well, think of that. And how m . . . that is . . . well, is the little lambie well taken care of?

GRANNY. Yes, Demmie. Jim left fifteen thousand dollars.

DEMETRIA. Fifteen thou . . . ! Dear little lambie. . . . Well, Nellie, maybe you're right.

GRANNY. About what ——?

DEMETRIA. Maybe I should adopt Pud.

GRANNY. Adopt him . . . ?

DEMETRIA. I mean if he has fifteen thousand dollars, I could give him some of the things he's been used to.

GRANNY. Yes, but adopt him . . . I didn't exactly mean . . . well, you wouldn't really have to adopt him, would you, Demmie? I just thought he'd sort of live over there with you and see Julian in the afternoons maybe and you could kind of . . . No. I guess not, Demmie. . . . I mean, Julian and I better . . .

DEMETRIA. I see. You mean you are going to go on letting Julian bring Pud up like a heathen.

GRANNY. Oh, I don't know what to do, Demmie. I'm so tired. (MARCIA *enters* D. L. *with glass of soda water, crosses to table* U. C. *above* GRANNY.)

MARCIA. Would you like some more soda, Mrs. Northrup?

GRANNY. Yes, I would, Marcy. Still feel a little rumbly down there.

MARCIA. Good afternoon, Miss Riffle.

DEMETRIA. (*Coldly.*) Good afternoon. (MARCIA *crosses* D. L. *off.* MARCIA *goes out bewildered.* DEMETRIA *leans over table after* MARCIA *is off.*) You don't mean to tell me you've got that Marcia Giles in this house.

GRANNY. (MARCIA *on* D. L. *from kitchen, crosses* R. *below porch, and off* D. R. *door.*) She came in to help us after the funeral. Why? Good straight-forward girl, isn't she? (DEMETRIA *crosses* L. C. *to* GRANNY.)

DEMETRIA. Well, her and that young Bill Murdock, Reverend Murdock's son . . .

GRANNY. Well, yes, Demmie . . . what about them?

DEMETRIA. Carrying on! Just as brazen as you please! (GRAMPS *on* R. *with dead frog above tree. Crosses* L. *to door* R., *enters house.*) And you're allowing a person like that to be around where Pud is. Nellie Northrup!

GRANNY. But I didn't know about it, Demmie.

DEMETRIA. You could've asked me. (GRAMPS *crosses* C. *to* DEMETRIA. *Pokes frog at her. Crosses* U. R. *Holds.*)

GRAMPS. Dead frog! Brand new. Beautiful specimen. Pud just found it.

DEMETRIA. How perfectly disgusting!

GRAMPS. Oh, don't feel that way, Demmie. We're gonna put *you* right up there next to him some day.

GRANNY. Julian! (*Gets book at desk.*)

GRAMPS. In a hurry, Miss Nellie. (*Holds* R. C.) Pud's waitin' for me under the barn. He just found a new mushroom. (*Thumbs through book.*) Think we got a Pleaurotus Ostreatus!

GRANNY. (*Crossing to* R. *of table.*) Julian, be careful. That may be a toadstool!

GRAMPS. (*Crossing to door, still thumbing through book.*) Well, that's what we're gonna find out.

DEMETRIA. (*Whispering to* GRANNY.) Marcia!

GRANNY. Julian, wait a minute.

GRAMPS. (*Going to her.*) What is it, Miss Nellie?

GRANNY. It's Marcia. I'm afraid we'll have to get rid of her. It seems she's carrying on with young Bill Murdock.

GRAMPS. Bill Murdock? Good. Nice boy, Bill.

DEMETRIA. (*Working* L. C.) And you're willing to have that kind of girl in your own home?

GRAMPS. What do you mean—that kind of a girl?

DEMETRIA. Why, she's nothing more than a common, little ——

GRAMPS. You're a liar!

GRANNY. Julian, don't you talk that way to Demmie. We don't know anything about Marcia.

GRAMPS. I know about her. Knew she was a nice girl the minute I saw her.

GRANNY. Demmie knows what she's talking about.

GRAMPS. (*To* DEMETRIA.) What do you know? Just tell me one thing!

DEMETRIA. All right. I saw them—right in the park.

GRAMPS. And what were they doin'? Right in the park.

DEMETRIA. Kissin'! Kissin'—like you never saw. Fair make your blood boil. If they carry on like that in public, what must they do when they're alone?

GRANNY. Well, but, Demmie—maybe they just kiss.

GRAMPS. Ye Gods—*that makes me mad!* That makes me so damn mad . . .

GRANNY. Julian Northrup, you stop your swearing! You stop your swearing!

GRAMPS. Miss Nellie, if you listen to another word this old hellion says you're just a plain fool!

GRANNY. (*Shakes finger at* GRAMPS.) Don't you call me a fool, Julian Northrup, don't you call me a fool! (GRANNY *collapses in chair,* DEMETRIA *above her.*)

GRAMPS. (*Roaring louder.*) I'm disappointed in you, Miss Nellie, I'm disappointed in you!

GRANNY. Oh, dear! Oh, dear!

DEMETRIA. There, now. You've tired yourself all out. I never should have told you about Marcia. It's all my fault.

GRANNY. You did just right, Demmie, you did just right. (GRAMPS *out door* R. *Sits porch* C.)

GRAMPS. Damned old hellion! Even makes me fight with Miss Nellie!

GRANNY. (DEMETRIA *holds about* GRANNY.) He can't call me a fool, Demmie. He can't say he's disappointed in me.

DEMETRIA. I don't see why you stand for it, Nellie. (*Gives* GRANNY *knitting.*) Now, here's your knitting.—Are you going to speak to Marcia?

GRANNY. Well, I don't know—if you just saw them kissin'.

DEMETRIA. Nellie!

GRANNY. All right, Demmie. Call to her. Ask her to make me a cup of tea. (DEMETRIA *goes off* L.)

MARCIA. (MARCIA *on* D. R. *crosses* C. *to* GRAMPS.) Mr. Northrup, Pud's yelling for you —— (*Starts out.*)

GRAMPS. Come here. (GRAMPS *crosses* D. R. C. *to* MARCIA.) What the devil do you mean by kissing men in the park?

MARCIA. What?

GRAMPS. Don't you know it's a sin for a girl to kiss men in the park?

MARCIA. But—but I didn't—I didn't kiss men in the park! I only kissed one man in the park.

GRAMPS. What'd you kiss him in the park for?

MARCIA. (*Nearly crying.*) Because we were in the park and . . .

GRAMPS. Well, next time you bring him up here and kiss him!

MARCIA. Wh-what?

GRAMPS. I say, you bring that Bill Murdock up here and kiss him.

'Stime we had a little kissin' in this house again. How the hell's Pud gonna learn about kissin' if he don't never see any of it?

MARCIA. Oh, Mr. Northrup! (*Throws arms around* GRAMPS, *begins to cry.*)

GRAMPS. (*Softer.*) There, there, Marcy. You in love with him?

MARCIA. Yes, oh, yes. We've been engaged all summer now.

GRAMPS. Yep. I thought I recognized the symptoms.

MARCIA. Bill's only got one more year at Law School and then we're gonna be married. He took highest honors in his class last year.

GRAMPS. Well, you just tell that to Miss Nellie and everything'll be all right. And the next time you and Bill meet Demetria in the park you make Bill give you a big smacker right in front of her. (GRAMPS *kisses* MARCIA. *Then she crosses* L.) Just like this.

DEMETRIA. (*Enters* D. L. *Crosses* R. C.) She's not here! Must be outside —— (DEMETRIA *on* D. L. *crosses* R. *above table to door* R. *Leans out. Calls.*) Marcia! (PUD *on* D. R. MARCIA *crosses* L. C. DEMETRIA *at door* R. *of house.*)

MARCIA. Yes, Miss Riffle.

DEMETRIA. Mrs. Northrup wants you to make her a cup of tea. And she has something to say to you.

MARCIA. (*Looks at* GRAMPS.) All right, Miss Riffle. (MARCIA *crosses* C. *on porch.* DEMETRIA *sits chair* R. *Gets tatting.*)

GRAMPS. (GRAMPS *beckons* MARCIA. *She crosses* D. R. *to him.*) You just tell Miss Nellie that you and Bill are engaged and that Bill got highest honors in his class.

MARCIA. All right. (MARCIA *crosses* U. C. *to door* R. *of house. Holds.*) Mr. Northrup.

GRAMPS. Huh?

MARCIA. Bill only got next to highest honors in his class.

GRAMPS. Tell her he got next to highest honors. Next to highest's good enough—damn it. (MARCIA *crosses* L. *above table. Off* D. L. GRAMPS *stands looking after her, chuckling.*) Real sweet girl, Marcy.

PUD. (*Looking after* MARCIA.) Gee, I wish Granny would knit two bumps on the front of my sweater the way Marcy's got on hers.

GRAMPS. (*Turns to* PUD.) What? Hey there, you! None of that from you, young man. Not that there ain't something in what you say. (GRAMPS *and* PUD *off* D. R.)

GRANNY. Oh, but I hate to do it. She needs the money so bad.

DEMETRIA. There are some things more important than money, Nellie. (GRANNY *chair* L., DEMETRIA *chair* R.)

GRANNY. Well, maybe you're right. There. I'll just finish this mitten. I was makin' 'em for Jim but Julian can use 'em. And after my cup of tea, think I could drop off for a spell.

DEMETRIA. Just what you should do, Nellie.

GRANNY. Feel kinda funny. (*Pause.*) He don't mean all the things he says. He's just a rough-spoken man is all.

DEMETRIA. Who? Julian?

GRANNY. And he ain't a blasphemer either—not exactly. He never sneers at religion. He just don't have no interest in it.

DEMETRIA. Amounts to the same thing. (*Sees* GRANNY *is dozing.*) Nellie dear, do you think I should take Pud's things over with me now?

GRANNY. (*Sleepily.*) Pud's things?

DEMETRIA. Yes. And in the morning, I'll go down to Mr. Pilbeam's and have the papers drawn up for you to sign—about the will and the adoption—and all. . . .

GRANNY. (*With a start.*) Now, see here, Demmie—I didn't say anything about your adoptin' Pud. You're trying to put words in my mouth. I don't like the way you're actin', Demmie.

DEMETRIA. Nellie Northrup, you said five minutes ago that I should bring Pud up.

GRANNY. I just wondered about it, Demmie.

DEMETRIA. You said it, Nellie. (BOY *on* R. *climbs tree.*)

GRANNY. If I did, I was wrong. I can see that now. . . . I don't like the way you're actin', Demmie. (*Falls back, weakly.*) Oh, dear. (DEMETRIA *crosses to her.*)

DEMETRIA. There, now, Nellie, don't think about it any more.

GRANNY. Ask Julian to come here, Demmie. I want to see him. (DEMETRIA *crosses* U. R. *Puts tatting on desk. Looks out door* R.)

DEMETRIA. There! There's a boy going up that apple tree!

GRANNY. Apples nice and ripe now.

DEMETRIA. Those nasty brats deserve a good whipping. Stealing other people's property! (DEMETRIA *crosses* R. *to door.*)

GRANNY. Julian never catches 'em. He starts bellowin' to give 'em plenty of time to get away.

DEMETRIA. (DEMETRIA *gives* L. *to* GRANNY.) Well, I bet I can catch 'em! Nasty little thief. . . .

GRANNY. (DEMETRIA *holds door, then out* R.) And don't forget to tell Julian to step in a minute. . . . (DEMETRIA *is already out of room, off porch, in front of tree.* GRANNY *hums, tries to knit, then drowses off.*)

DEMETRIA. Come down out of there. I see you.

BOY. (*In tree.*) I'm not doing anything. I just . . .

DEMETRIA. You're just a thief, that's what you are.

BOY. I didn't take any apples.

DEMETRIA. You good-for-nothing, you come down from there this minute.

BOY. I can't.

DEMETRIA. You got up all right.

BOY. My pants is caught in behind.

DEMETRIA. Either you come down this minute, or I'll have the law on you.

BOY. (*Crying.*) I'm not doing anything. I didn't take any apples yet. . . .

DEMETRIA. You come down from there. I'll teach you to trespass. (GRAMPS *and* PUD *on* D. R. GRAMPS *crosses* R. C. *to* DEMETRIA. GRAMPS *carries a stick.*)

GRAMPS. (DEMETRIA *turns.*) You'll do what?

DEMETRIA. (*Defensively.*) There's a boy up that tree.

GRAMPS. And what were you goin' to teach him?

DEMETRIA. I should think you'd thank me to catch a trespasser for you.

GRAMPS. And how was you figurin' to teach him not to trespass?

DEMETRIA. (*Looking at* BOY.) I'd give him a good sound whipping, that's what I'd do.

GRAMPS. You would. (*Raises stick.*) Thanks for tellin' me, Demmie. Because seein' as how there happens to be two trespassers here, I'll just begin with the one that's handiest. (GRAMPS *crosses* C. DEMETRIA *gives* L.)

DEMETRIA. Oh, don't be so silly, Julian.

PUD. (*Jumping up and down.*) Hit her, Gramps. Hit her on the rump!

DEMETRIA. Why . . . you little brat.

GRAMPS. (*Waving stick.*) You git off my property! (DEMETRIA *crosses* C. *on porch.*)

DEMETRIA. All right, Julian Northrup! Maybe you'll find out whose property this is some day!

GRAMPS. You'll find out I can take care of my own.

DEMETRIA. Sometimes the law has something to say about things. (DEMETRIA *off* R. *end porch. Crosses* U. C. *and off to* L. GRAMPS *puts stick on* R. *end porch.* PUD *holds* D. R.)

GRAMPS. (*Looking in tree.*) Whose boy are you?

BOY. Jud Martin.

GRAMPS. Why're you stealin' my apples?

BOY. I'm hungry.

GRAMPS. Don't your folks give you nothin' to eat?

BOY. Yes, sir.

GRAMPS. So you're apple-hungry?

BOY. Yes, sir.

GRAMPS. Why don't you come down?

BOY. I can't.

GRAMPS. Why can't you?

BOY. My breeches is caught.

GRAMPS. Your breeches is caught.

PUD. (*Jumping up and down, excitedly.*) Gramps, Gramps! Your wish! He can't come down! (PUD *and* GRAMPS *work* C. *and* L. C.) He can't come down! He can't come down!

GRAMPS. Ssh! (*To* BOY.) Now, you unloosen your breeches. (BOY *tugs again at breeches, finds they are loose.*) And come down from there as fast as you can.

BOY. (*Bewildered.*) Yes, sir. I'm coming. My breeches is loose now. (BOY *climbs down. Holds* D. R. C.)

PUD. Aw, Gramps, you shouldn't have let him unloose his breeches. We could of kept him up there for a million years.

GRAMPS. Now, would that have been nice, son? (GRAMPS *crosses* U. R. *above tree. Takes 2 apples. Crosses* D. R. *Puts in* BOY'S *pants pockets.*) Now then, I'll teach you to steal. Here. Here. The next time you want apples, don't sneak around the back. Walk right up to the front door, ring the bell and ask for some. Will you do that?

BOY. Yes, sir!

PUD. Like heck he will. (PUD *attacks* BOY. *Tussle.* BOY *gets* PUD *down and sits on him.*)

GRAMPS. You fellows stop that! Pud, you lay off that boy. (*Boys up.* GRAMPS *shoves* BOY U. R. C.) Go along, you.

BOY. Thanks, Mr. Northrup. (BOY *off* U. R.)

PUD. Gramps, what'd you stop us for? I had him practical licked.

GRAMPS. Yes, I guess you did. . . . Them apples I gave him'll be pretty bitter, 'cause he didn't steal them. (PUD *crosses* R. C. *to down side tree.*)

PUD. Boost me up, Gramps. Boost me up.

GRAMPS. Boost you up! (GRAMPS *crosses* R. *to* PUD. *Helps him up. Gives* R. C.) You don't have to steal. Oh, all right. By golly, boy, you're a full-time job. . . . Now, you're up!

PUD. (*In tree, shakes finger at* GRAMPS.) Now, you know I can't get down until you let me.

GRAMPS. (*Laughs.*) My Lord and Miss Boopydoop, you sure do beat the trolley cars.

PUD. You wished *nobody* could come down until you let them. That was your wish.

GRAMPS. That's right, boy. Guess it was.

PUD. So I can't come down either. I hope you won't keep me up here too long, Gramps.

GRAMPS. Liable to keep you up there all week. Maybe a hundred years. Depends on how I feel.

PUD. Oh, no, Gramps.

GRAMPS. Yep. (GRAMPS *off* D. R. *ad libbing.* MARCIA *on* D. L. *with tea tray. Crosses* C., *puts tray on table. Holds* R. *of table. Fixes inkpot, arranges dishes, etc.*)

MARCIA. Here's your tea, Mrs. Northrup.

GRANNY. (*Faintly.*) Oh, just set it down, Marcy.

MARCIA. (*Frightened.*) Is there anything wrong, Mrs. Northrup?

GRANNY. Wrong? No, there's nothing wrong, Marcy. I'm just kind of tired. I'm goin' to go to sleep in a minute. . . . Now, let me see, there was somethin' I was supposed to talk to you about! Now, what was it? . . . Well, there, I've forgotten. Couldn't have been very important. (*Pause.*) Marcy!

MARCIA. Yes, Mrs. Northrup? (MARCIA *above* GRANNY.)

GRANNY. (*Takes* MARCIA's *hand.*) Marcy—you just see that Julian always has his pipe. Will you do that?

MARCIA. (*Bewildered.*) Yes, Mrs. Northrup.

GRANNY. You're a good girl, Marcy. Now, go on back to whatever you're doin'. (MARCIA *off* D. L., *then* BRINK *on from* R. *arch. Holds door.*)

BRINK. (*Approaching her.*) Don't you think you have done enough?

GRANNY. That you, Julian?

BRINK. No, not Julian.

GRANNY. Who is it?

BRINK. It's Mr. Brink. You seem rather tired.

GRANNY. I am kinda tired, Mr. Brink.

BRINK. I thought so. Well, you're to come with me now.

GRANNY. (*Rousing.*) Come with you? Brink? I don't know any . . . See here, what call have you to come buttin' in here?

BRINK. I usually come to bedrooms. It's so much more comfortable.

GRANNY. What is?

BRINK. To come with me.

GRANNY. Why should anyone go with you?

BRINK. It's customary.

GRANNY. Oh? Well, you might as well sit down and wait. Because you needn't think I'll stir until I've finished this mitten. (*Confidentially.*) I'm narrowin' off at the top now.

BRINK. Yes, I know you are.

GRANNY. (*Laughs.*) What do you know about knittin'?

BRINK. I don't mean the mitten. I mean you.

GRANNY. (*Laughs.*) What a fool thing to say. Don't you know a lady from a mitten?

BRINK. (*Turns* L.) Yes, I know a lady from a mitten.

GRANNY. Now, don't go 'way. You'll just have to wait. I've got to finish this job for my son, Jim. . . . (*Puzzled for a moment, then nods to affirm statement.*) When he drives to Gainesville he says there won't anythin' keep his hands warm but a pair of my mittens. (*Laughs.*) Those boughten things you get at the store—they're no good. A doctor has to be out in all kinds of weather, you know.

BRINK. (*Smiling.*) He won't need them this year.

GRANNY. (*Laughs.*) Huh! What do you know about it?

BRINK. Oh, I know many things.

GRANNY. I'll wager I could show you a thing or two about knittin'.

BRINK. (*Crossing close to her.*) No doubt. Are you ready now?

GRANNY. (*Breathlessly.*) Wait . . . just a minute . . . I'm almost finished . . . (*Breaks thread.*) There! That's got it! Don't that red stripe look well with the gray?

BRINK. Excellent, my dear. Excellent. (BRINK *extends* L. *arm. Holds till* GRANNY *dies.*) Come now. (*She smiles and dies. Enter* GRAMPS D. R., *whistling. Crosses* C., *looks up at* PUD, *who has remained quietly in tree on* U. S. *side during* GRANNY'S *death scene.*)

GRAMPS. Might leave you there and go down to Milbaur Park and pick up a few new specimens for our collection.

PUD. (*Starts to climb large branch.*) Then I'm coming down, Gramps.

GRAMPS. But you can't. You're under my magic spell. Yep, think I'll go along right now . . . good-bye. (*Rises.*)

PUD. Wait a minute. I'm coming with you. (PUD *climbs to out* L. *limb of tree, hangs there.*) Gramps, I can't let loose!

GRAMPS. 'Course you can't. You can't let loose till I tell you.

PUD. (*Frightened.*) But, honest, I can't, Gramps.

GRAMPS. (*Thundering.*) 'Course you can't. You can't go breaking my spells like that!

PUD. (*More frightened.*) Let me down, Gramps! Let me down! Please! My arms is tired! (GRAMPS *laughs.*) Gramps! Gramps! Let me go, let me go! Gramps! Gramps!

GRAMPS. Come on, then. Let go. Let go, honey. (PUD *drops to ground. Runs* C. *to* GRAMPS.) What's the matter, boy, what's the matter?

PUD. (*Wailing.*) I couldn't let go!

GRAMPS. Of course you could.

PUD. No, I couldn't, Gramps. My hands wouldn't move!

GRAMPS. I thought we were just foolin'.

PUD. I was foolin' at first and then my hands wouldn't move. The tree was holdin' me. (*Looks up at tree.*)

GRAMPS. By golly, you do give a person the creeps sometimes. Dog-gone if I don't believe you really thought that tree was holdin' you.

PUD. It was, Gramps, it was.

GRAMPS. Oh, that old apple tree couldn't hold anybody!

PUD. (*Turning, pointing at* GRAMPS.) Yes, it could, Gramps. You wished it could. (GRAMPS *and* PUD *off* R. *above tree.* MARCIA *on* D. L., *crosses* C. *toward* R. *door, sees* GRANNY, *stops short, understands what has happened.*)

MARCIA. (*Crying.*) Mr. Northrup! (*Crosses* R. *to door.*) Come quick! Mr. Northrup! . . . Mr. Northrup! (*Kneels by* GRANNY.)

CURTAIN

ACT I

SCENE 3

A week later. Nearly dusk.

AT RISE: GRAMPS *sits alone* C. *edge porch. Moody. Wears mourning band on arm.* MARCIA *on* U. C., *crosses* R. *through room—out door* R. *Crosses* C. *to* GRAMPS *on porch,* R. *of him.*

MARCIA. (*Carrying mixing bowl.*) Mr. Northrup.
GRAMPS. (*Looking up.*) Oh, hello there, Marcy.
MARCIA. Supper's nearly ready. Time you got washed.
GRAMPS. All right, Marcy.
MARCIA. Miss Riffle was just over again.
GRAMPS. Was she?
MARCIA. She's been over every day since the funeral. She keeps asking about your health.
GRAMPS. Damned old hellion. Just waitin' for me to die, ain't she?
MARCIA. Oh, Mr. Northrup. You've got to take care of yourself. If you don't eat any more than you have the last week . . . (MARCIA *crosses down on ground to* GRAMPS.) You've got to keep up your strength, Mr. Northrup.
GRAMPS. All right, Marcy. Thank you. (*Doesn't move.*)
MARCIA. And Pud seems awfully lonesome lately, too.
GRAMPS. Pud?
MARCIA. He doesn't seem himself at all.
GRAMPS. That so?
MARCIA. When you don't eat, he hardly eats a mouthful either.
Group 1
GRAMPS. That's what she said. She said "he mimics everything you do."
MARCIA. That's right. He does.
GRAMPS. (*Suddenly.*) If I'd only got there in time, Marcy!
MARCIA. (*Sits* R. *of* GRAMPS.) Oh, don't take it so hard, Mr. Northrup.
GRAMPS. We had words and she died before I could take 'em back and say I was sorry.
MARCIA. She understood!
GRAMPS. She died and she didn't forgive me, she died and she didn't forgive me.

MARCIA. She did, Mr. Northrup. She would have forgiven you for anything. . . . Oh, I almost forgot . . . (MARCIA *off through door* D. L. *Crosses* U. C. *room and off to* L. *arch.* PUD *enters* D. R.)

PUD. Gramps!

GRAMPS. Oh, hello there, sonny. (PUD *crosses* U. R. *to* GRAMPS.)

PUD. Shall I sit down here too?

GRAMPS. Sure thing. What makes you think you shouldn't?

PUD. I think I should. (PUD *sits* R. *of* GRAMPS.)

GRAMPS. Gonna have supper in a minute.

PUD. I'm not hungry.

GRAMPS. Gotta eat, boy. Hungry or not hungry.

PUD. Why?

GRAMPS. Keep up your strength. (*Suddenly clutches* PUD.) There's only me and you left now. Only me and you. I figure we got to stick together.

PUD. You're damn right.

GRAMPS. Shouldn't cuss, boy.

PUD. Why shouldn't I? *You* say that.

GRAMPS. I shouldn't neither. Your Granny didn't like it. Let's you and me turn over a new leaf, Pud.

PUD. What for?

GRAMPS. So your Aunt Demmie won't keep on saying I'm bad for you and won't keep on trying to get you away from me.

PUD. Aw, we'll kill her.

GRAMPS. By the Lord Harry, I almost wish we could.

PUD. (*Excited.*) We'll kill her; we'll kill her and we'll put her in the ground. We'll lower the coffing and I'll say . . .

GRAMPS. Hush, boy. Hush! (*Leans down, puts head in hands.*)

PUD. (*Touching him.*) What's the matter, Gramps? Are you sick? (MARCIA *enters through arch. Crosses* D. L. *through kitchen and enters forestage through* L. *screen door.* D. L. *of* GRAMPS *witn pipe.*)

GRAMPS. Growin' pains, I guess.

MARCIA. Here's your pipe, Mr. Northrup.

GRAMPS. My pipe, Marcy? Oh, I don't believe I can smoke it, thank you kindly. My throat hurts me a little. Fact is, I don't think I'll ever smoke any more. She didn't like it.

MARCIA. But she did, Mr. Northrup. I know she did.

GRAMPS. Nope. Miss Nellie thought it was a dirty habit. And I guess it is. . . .

MARCIA. She told me I was always to keep your pipe filled.

GRAMPS. Miss Nellie what? When?

MARCIA. Just before she died. (*Sits* L. *of* GRAMPS.) I took her up a cup of tea and she caught hold of my hand and said . . . wait, I'll remember her exact words . . . she said: "Marcy . . . Marcy, see that Julian always has his pipe."

GRAMPS. Marcy. . . . You're not just making this up to make me feel good?

MARCIA. No, no, Mr. Northrup. I couldn't do that. (*Holds up pipe.*)

GRAMPS. Give me the pipe. (GRAMPS *starts pipe.* MARCIA *rises, takes match from him, lights pipe.*)

PUD. Does it taste good, Gramps?

GRAMPS. Better'n anything I know, boy.

MARCIA. I'll go finish supper. (MARCIA *off* D. L.)

PUD. Why did your hand wiggle so when you lighted the pipe, Gramps?

GRAMPS. Did it, sonny? Guess I haven't been keepin' up my strength. Do feel kind of shaky. . . . (GRAMPS *nods.* BRINK *on* R. *of tree holds* R. C., *branches of tree across him.* GRAMPS *swings* PUD *to his* L. *on seeing* BRINK.)

BRINK. Good evening.

GRAMPS. Oh, it's you, is it? What do you want?

BRINK. You.

GRAMPS. Can't I ever shut my eyes without you buttin' in?

BRINK. I thought perhaps you'd like to come with me now.

GRAMPS. Now look here, Mr. Brink. I ain't goin' with you at all. I'm goin' to stay right here with this young fellow. And you're about as welcome as a fly on a currant bun, so now you know.

BRINK. Your similitudes are a trifle earthy, but your meaning is clear.

GRAMPS. (*Turns to* PUD, *laughs.*) My similitudes! What kind of talk is that?

PUD. Sure. What kind of talk is that! He sure talks funny, doesn't he, Gramps?

GRAMPS. Now go on. Get off my property!

BRINK. Now, let's not be difficult about it. Your wife was so charming to me.

GRAMPS. Miss Nellie? Is she well?

BRINK. Sorry. I can't tell you that. Only that she has changed.

GRAMPS. Miss Nellie changed? That's what you think!
BRINK. Oh, my dear man, let's not argue the point, and this time you can't fight me away. (*Pause.*) Come now.
GRAMPS. No, no—I ——
BRINK. Come now. Come.
GRAMPS. No. No. (GRAMPS *is stricken with pain. Looks at* PUD.)
BRINK. You're being difficult again. It's so easy and so pleasant. Now don't worry. Look at me. (BRINK *reaches* L. *arm to* GRAMPS.)
GRAMPS. Just a minute, please, Mr. Brink. I'd like to have one last apple before I go.
BRINK. Oh, all right. (GRAMPS *rises, crosses* R. *to tree, reaches up —holds.*)
GRAMPS. You wouldn't like to get it for me, would you?
BRINK. Curious request. Oh, why not? (BRINK *climbs tree from* U. *side, points to apples* R. *and* L. *Holds.* GRAMPS *and* PUD *hold* C.) This one? Or this one?
GRAMPS. I don't want none of them! I got you up that tree and you're gonna stay there until I tell you to come down. (*Wind shakes tree, as* BRINK *struggles to get free. Is bewildered.*)
PUD. (*Puttings arms around* GRAMPS.) You got him, Gramps. You got him! (*Light flickers. Thunder. Tree shakes.* GRAMPS *clutches* PUD, *looks at him.*)
GRAMPS. By golly, boy, I believe we have!

CURTAIN

ACT II

SCENE 1

Two hours later. It is dusk. A fence is being built around the tree. On curtain two WORKMEN *pounding* U. R. *above tree.*

AT RISE: DEMETRIA *enters* D. L. *door. Holds* L. *end porch. Goes to* WORKMEN. BRINK *is invisible in tree.*

DEMETRIA. (*To* WORKMEN.) Here you, come here.
WORKMAN. (*Crossing* C. *to her.*) Yes, ma'am.
DEMETRIA. Has Mr. Northrup told any of you men why he's building this fence?
WORKMAN. Well, not exactly, ma'am. It's to keep people away from the tree.
DEMETRIA. Why?
WORKMAN. He says if we touch the tree we are in danger.
DEMETRIA. Danger of what?
WORKMAN. Well, I'm not sure, ma'am, I thought he said we were in danger of our lives.
DEMETRIA. That's very interesting. That's what he said to me too. (1ST WORKMAN *crosses* R. C. *and off* R., *followed by* 2ND WORKMAN. *Enter* EVANS *and* PILBEAM. EVANS *and* PILBEAM *cross* C. *porch.* DEMETRIA *holds* L. C. *porch.*) Ah, Doctor Evans, Mr. Pilbeam, how do you do? I'm glad you could come. Julian is out by the garage burying his dog.
EVANS. (*Going to her down* C.) What does he want us for?
DEMETRIA. He doesn't want you, gentlemen. It was I who asked you to come up. I want you to meet someone.
PILBEAM. (R. *of* DEMETRIA.) Who? (*Steps on.*)
DEMETRIA. A friend of Julian's—a Mr. Brink.
EVANS. I'm rather busy right now, Miss Riffle. (EVANS *gives* C.)
DEMETRIA. I appreciate that, Doctor, but I thought you would like to meet this friend of Julian's.
EVANS. (*Looks at watch. Puts satchel* D. R. *end porch.*) Well, all right, where is he?

DEMETRIA. Well, just at the moment, he's up in the apple tree. (*Pause. They look at her surprised, then look up into tree.* DEMETRIA *stands watching them in silence.*)
PILBEAM. (*To her.*) Er—where did you say he was?
DEMETRIA. Right up in that apple tree. (EVANS *and* PILBEAM *cross* D. R. C. *Look in tree.*)
EVANS. I don't see anyone up there.
DEMETRIA. Oh, no. You can't see him. He's invisible.
PILBEAM. What? (EVANS *and* PILBEAM *cross* C. *to* DEMETRIA. *She crosses* D. L. C.)
DEMETRIA. He's invisible.—You see, a short while after Julian got Mr. Brink up there, Betty, the old dog, saw him and barked at him. Mr. Brink didn't like that so he became invisible. And right after that, Betty touched her nose to the tree and dropped over dead. Julian and Pud are burying her now.
EVANS. What is this anyway? (EVANS *crosses* C. *to* DEMETRIA.)
PILBEAM. Is this supposed to be a joke, Miss Riffle?
DEMETRIA. What would you say if I told you I believed it was the Gospel truth?
EVANS. 'Fraid I'd say you were crazy.
DEMETRIA. I would be crazy, wouldn't I? And what if I told you that Mr. Brink is a man, just like you, who goes around taking people away with him when it's time for them to die. Now, if I believed that you'd surely say I was crazy, wouldn't you?
EVANS. I'd say you were positively nuts, Miss Riffle.
DEMETRIA. Yes. (EVANS *and* PILBEAM *turn* R. C.) Well, I don't believe it—(EVANS *and* PILBEAM *turn to* DEMETRIA.) but Julian does.
PILBEAM. Come, come, Miss Riffle, what kind of story is this?
DEMETRIA. An hour ago when I happened to be passing, I saw all these pieces of fence being unloaded from a truck. Naturally, I came back to find out what was going on. Julian told me he was building the fence to keep people away from the tree, because anybody who touched the tree would die.
PILBEAM. Die?
DEMETRIA. And not only that! Touching that tree is the only way anyone can die. There is no more death in the world, Mr. Pilbeam, until Julian lets Mr. Brink come down.
EVANS. See here, Miss Riffle, you don't think Northrup really believes this?

DEMETRIA. Julian is an old man and he's been through a great deal lately. I think it's perfectly obvious what has happened. His mind has just suddenly snapped. Julian Northrup is as crazy as a loon.

EVANS. No, no, I saw Northrup only day before yesterday. He was as sane as any man could be. He's just an old joker. I've known him for years. (EVANS *crosses* D. R.)

DEMETRIA. You have, Doctor Evans. And Mr. Pilbeam has been his lawyer for years. That's why I've asked both of you to come up. I'm not asking you to take my word for it. I'm simply asking you to see Julian and convince yourselves that what I'm saying is true.

PILBEAM. (*With a look to* EVANS.) If Northrup should be insane, you'd have to take Pud, of course, wouldn't you, Miss Riffle?

DEMETRIA. Naturally. I'm next of kin.

EVANS. Huh!

PILBEAM. That's what I thought. (EVANS *crosses* R. C. *above tree.* PILBEAM *crosses* D. R.)

DEMETRIA. What do you mean? You don't think I'm making this up about Julian? (EVANS *holds* R. *end porch. Starts to touch twig of tree, then draws back.*)

PILBEAM. I don't know what to think, Miss Riffle.

DEMETRIA. Ever since Nellie Northrup died, Mr. Pilbeam, you've tried to stop my adopting Pud. Even though I told you that was her dying wish.

PILBEAM. I simply said no court of law would believe you, Miss Riffle.

DEMETRIA. I guess a court of law will feel different about it, if they realize a young boy is being brought up by a maniac! I'll be frank with you, Mr. Pilbeam, I intend to get that boy away from this insane man's house before something terrible happens. (EVANS *crosses* L. *on porch.* 1ST *and* 2ND WORKMEN *on* R. *with up side fence.* 1ST WORKMAN *crosses* D. R. C. *close to* R. *end porch and tree.*) Tonight—if possible! (DEMETRIA *crosses* U. C. *porch to* EVANS.) There is a way of taking care of such cases immediately, isn't there?

EVANS. Well, yes. I'll tell you, I'm not a psychiatrist, Miss Riffle, but if I think Northrup's crazy, I'll talk it over with Grimes. He's the head of the asylum.

DEMETRIA. You will talk it over with him tonight?

EVANS. (*Crossly.*) When a person's insane you don't usually let him run around loose.

DEMETRIA. Thank you, Doctor Evans, I'll just ask the workmen to . . . (GRAMPS *is heard bellowing off stage.* GRAMPS *and* PUD *on* D. R., PUD *with spade. Hold* D. R.)

GRAMPS. Here you, there. What the hell do you mean by gettin' so near to that tree? Didn't I tell you to stay away from that tree on peril of your lives?

PUD. (*Carries spade.*) What the hell's the idea?

GRAMPS. (*Still to* WORKMEN.) Now, you fellows, go on back to that truck and get the rest of that fence unloaded. Get a move on.

PUD. Get a move on. (PUD *leans spade* D. R. *below door. Both* WORKMEN *off* R. *above tree.* GRAMPS *moves* C. PUD *sits ground below horse.*)

GRAMPS. Now, what in tarnation are you doin' around here again! I told you . . .

DEMETRIA. It's just that I'm so excited about it, Julian.

GRAMPS. And Pilbeam and Evans, eh? By God, you've told them all about it, haven't you? After I told you not to.

DEMETRIA. Why, no, Julian, I haven't told. . . .

EVANS. (PILBEAM *crosses* D. C. *to* GRAMPS.) Yes, she's told us all about it. About the tree, the fence, Mr. Brink . . . everything.

GRAMPS. I might have known it. I might have known it.

EVANS. Well, what about it, Northrup? What's the answer?

GRAMPS. Well, it's the truth, Evans. It's just as true as I'm standin' here.

PILBEAM. (*Laughing.* PILBEAM *crosses a step to* GRAMPS.) You mean there's somebody sitting up in that tree?

EVANS. And nobody in the world can die any more?

GRAMPS. Nobody can die any more until I say so, unless they touch that tree, or one of them apples, or Mr. Brink himself.

EVANS. You're not serious about this, Northrup?

DEMETRIA. (*Down.* DEMETRIA *crosses* D. L. C. *and nudges* EVANS.) Of course he is, Doctor. He's perfectly serious, aren't you, Julian?

GRAMPS. (*Crosses* C. *to* DEMETRIA.) Hey there, what the hell are you up to anyway?

DEMETRIA. Why, nothing, Julian. I'm just interested. . . .

GRAMPS. Well, I don't want you to go telling anybody else about Mr. Brink. (GRAMPS *sits* R. *on horse.*) I got him up there and now I gotta figure out what the hell I'm gonna do with him.

DEMETRIA. But you don't think you'll be able to keep a thing like this quiet, Julian.

EVANS. Look here, Northrup. Can you talk to Mr. Brink?

GRAMPS. Sure I can talk to him.

EVANS. Have you talked to him since you got him up there?

GRAMPS. Nope. Haven't had time.

EVANS. I wish you'd talk to him now.

GRAMPS. What for? Just so's you can hear him?

EVANS. I just thought, perhaps if you tried to talk to him—well, you'd find out he isn't up there any more.

GRAMPS. Oh, he's up there, all right.

DEMETRIA. Julian, do try to make him talk. (MARCIA *on* U. L. *house from* L. *arch. Crosses* D. L. *out door* D. L. *Holds* L. *end porch.*) I'd love to hear him.

GRAMPS. Oh, you would. Well, by golly, Demmie. (GRAMPS *crosses* C. *Turns to tree.* EVANS *and* PILBEAM *give up.* DEMETRIA *to* EVANS.) I believe I'll let you. I'll let you all hear him. (GRAMPS *gives* R. *to tree.*) Mr. Brink, can you hear me if I don't shout?

BRINK. Sir?

GRAMPS. See, he calls me "Sir." . . .

DEMETRIA. (*To* EVANS *and* PILBEAM.) There, he thinks someone's answering.

GRAMPS. Well, Mr. Brink, I'm sorry I haven't had more of a chance to talk to you.

BRINK. Perhaps I shouldn't say it but I'm not extremely upset by that.

GRAMPS. You're not mad at me, are you?

BRINK. I think I might justifiably be allowed some slight irritation.

GRAMPS. Well, I wouldn't have put you there without a damn good reason. I got you up there so this old hellion couldn't get Pud and the money his father left him. (PILBEAM *sits* C. *edge porch.*)

BRINK. I appreciate that your motive was probably sincere.

GRAMPS. Now, I got an idea, and it's goin' to settle once and for all this business of her gettin' Pud. (GRAMPS *crosses* L. *to* DEMETRIA. *Pulls her* C., *facing tree.* GRAMPS *crosses to tree again.*) Come here, you. Stand out there. (*To* BRINK.) You see this old battle-ax here—her name is Demetria Riffle. Have you got anything on your schedule about when you are supposed to snuff her out?

BRINK. Riffle? There's no such name that has come to my attention yet.

GRAMPS. Well, Mr. Brink, I'm goin' to keep you up there until it's time for you to exterminate her.

BRINK. My dear man, that may be a very long time yet. There's no telling how long that woman may hang on.

GRAMPS. Well, that's the way it's goin' to be.

BRINK. But for me to stay here any length of time might be considered by my Superior as a considerable dereliction of duty.

GRAMPS. Can't help it. Them's the terms.

BRINK. (*With sigh.*) Ah, well! I was afraid of that. Very well, since you and your tree are so tenacious, I shall have to sit here and wait for Miss Riffle's call.

GRAMPS. Do you think you can hold out that long?

BRINK. My dear man, a human life is like the twinkling of an eye to me.

GRAMPS. Oh, yes, I suppose it is. All right, then, Mr. Brink. (GRAMPS *turns back to others and sits on horse.*) Well, there you you are! (*All look at him.*)

DEMETRIA. Julian, I'm sorry for you. I really am. (DEMETRIA *gives to* GRAMPS *a step.*)

GRAMPS. Sorry for me? You heard what Mr. Brink said, didn't you?

DEMETRIA. No—I—didn't hear this thing in the tree say anything.

GRAMPS. You didn't? You heard Mr. Brink, Pilbeam? (GRAMPS *rises. Crosses* R. C.)

PILBEAM. I'm sorry, Northrup. I didn't.

GRAMPS. (*To* EVANS.) Evans!

EVANS. No, Northrup, I didn't. . . .

GRAMPS. (*Frantically.*) Marcia! (MARCIA *turns away.*) Well, I'll be a . . . what the hell's the matter? (GRAMPS *sits horse.*) Am I goin' nuts?

EVANS. (EVANS *crosses* C. *to* GRAMPS.) It's probably just some sort of a dream or something, Northrup. You'll probably get over it in a few weeks and be all right again.

GRAMPS. (*Softly.*) Didn't no one hear what he said? (GRAMPS *rises.*)

PUD. (*Suddenly.* PUD *rises. Holds* R. *of* GRAMPS.) He said a human life was like the twinkling of an eye to him.

GRAMPS. Ye Gods, that's just what he said! Just what he said! A dream, eh? What clse did he say, Pud? (MARCIA *off door* D. L.)

PUD. Said he'd have to stay up there 'cause you and the tree was ten . . . ten . . . it was another funny word, Gramps.

GRAMPS. Tenacious!

DEMETRIA. (*To* EVANS *and* PILBEAM.) See what he's doing to the boy.

GRAMPS. That's just what he said. (GRAMPS *crosses* R. *Sits horse.*) You see where that leaves you. (*Pause.*)

DEMETRIA. Guess I'm too dull to hear.

GRAMPS. That's it. Must be. Guess you're all too dull to hear.

PILBEAM. Yes, I guess that must be it. (EVANS *crosses* D. L. *Holds. Turns to* GRAMPS. *They are strangely silent.*)

EVANS. I want to show you something, Northrup. (EVANS *crosses* R. C.)

GRAMPS. Hey, there, what are you goin' to do? (EVANS *crosses to tree.*)

EVANS. I'm going to eat an apple for you.

GRAMPS. Hey. (GRAMPS *trips* EVANS. EVANS *falls by* R. *end porch.* PUD *grabs spade.* GRAMPS *takes it, threatens* EVANS. PILBEAM *rises.*) You gol-darned fool, after all I've been tellin' you about them apples. You make one more move toward that tree and I'll brain you. (DEMETRIA *screams, hops up* L. *on porch.* EVANS *is on ground.*)

EVANS. (*Quietly.*) All right, Northrup. Let me up. I won't go near the tree.

GRAMPS. Gol-darn fool, tryin' to commit suicide!

EVANS. (*Rises.*) All right, Northrup. (GRAMPS *gives* PUD *spade.*) I just wanted to make sure you weren't joking. (*With look to others.*) Are you going to be home a little later this evening, Northrup?

GRAMPS. 'Course I am.

EVANS. I may be over and—er—talk some more about this.

GRAMPS. All right, Evans.

EVANS. Thanks, well . . . (EVANS *nods at* PILBEAM *and* DEMETRIA.)

DEMETRIA. I must go.

PILBEAM. Yes.—I'll go along with you —— (DEMETRIA *off up* R. C. *porch.* PILBEAM *follows her off* R. *porch.*)

EVANS. Good-bye, Northrup.

GRAMPS. Good-bye, Evans. Sorry I had to be rough with you.

EVANS. That's all right. (*Picks up bag—starts off* U. R. C. *grounds. Switches away from tree to porch.*)

GRAMPS. And don't worry about none of your patients dying for a while, yet.

EVANS. (*With a look at* GRAMPS.) All right. Good-bye, Northrup. (EVANS *off* U. R. C.)

GRAMPS. Well, now, back to work, sonny, back to work. (GRAMPS *and* PUD *start* U. R. *Hold* R. C. *by tree.*)

PUD. Why don't they hear Mr. Brink?

GRAMPS. Don't know, boy, guess they're all too busy.

BRINK. (*Appears.*) Oh, my dear man, that isn't the reason at all.

GRAMPS. (*Turning to him.*) Oh, hello, Mr. Brink. Why is it only Pud and me can hear you, then?

BRINK. I won't go into it now if you don't mind.

GRAMPS. Just as you say, Mr. Brink. One thing I would like to know though.

BRINK. Well?

GRAMPS. You don't think they'll hold it against Pud what I'm doin' to you?

BRINK. I have neither the inclination nor the authorization to dispense information relevant to your inquiry.

PUD. (*Laughs.*) He still talks funny.

GRAMPS. Well, guess I'll have to take that chance. Come on, boy. Say good-bye to Mr. Brink. (*Helps* PUD *up.*)

PUD. 'Bye, Brink.

GRAMPS. Can't you say " Mr. Brink "?

PUD. Good-bye, Mr. Brink—excuse me.

BRINK. That's all right—good-bye, Pud.

GRAMPS. Well, we gotta get that fence finished tonight, boy.

PUD. We gotta work like hell to do it, though, Gramps. (GRAMPS *and* PUD *off* U. R. C.)

CURTAIN

ACT II — fri

SCENE 2

Ten o'clock that night.

AT RISE: GRAMPS *is sleeping in chair* L. *of table with newspaper over his head.* PUD (D. R. *room*) *with a book, on floor.* 1ST *and* 2ND WORKMEN R. C. *above tree, pounding.*

PUD. (*Singing.*) The King of Massonia wore his crown upon his seat. (PUD *up, pulls paper off* GRAMPS' *head. Climbs up on his knees. Pause.*) Hey, Gramps.
GRAMPS. How's that?
PUD. The King of Massonia wore his crown on his seat.
GRAMPS. You don't say. And where did you learn that?
PUD. In Sunday school.
GRAMPS. Don't recall that particular passage myself, son. You don't, by any chance, mean the King of Macedonia, do you?
PUD. I guess I mean the King of Massachusetts.
GRAMPS. That's probably it. What did he wear his crown on his seat for?
PUD. He just wanted to sit on it. (WORKMEN *pound a bit* U. R., *then off* R.) They're doing a pretty good job on that fence, Gramps.
GRAMPS. Yep, they'll finish it before morning. (PUD *is on* GRAMPS' *knee, showing thumb, bound with adhesive tape.*) What on earth did you do to your thumb?
PUD. I hurt it when I was buildin' the fence. But Marcy put a heap o' tape on it, so I guess it's all right.
GRAMPS. (*Laughs.*) A heap o' tape. A heap o' tape. Yes, adhesive tape will fix anythin'.
PUD. Gramps, how long before Doctor Evans is coming over?
GRAMPS. Ought to be along any minute now. (PUD *leans head back on* GRAMPS' *shoulder, plays with his hair.*)
PUD. Sinkpea, sinkpea, sinkpea.
GRAMPS. How's that?
PUD. Sinkpea.
GRAMPS. What on earth is that?

PUD. Just sinkpea.
GRAMPS. Where'd you hear that word?
PUD. I thought of it myself. I was thinkin' of a boat sinkin', and of a pea, so I said—sinkpea.
GRAMPS. What more natural!
PUD. Say it, Gramps.
GRAMPS. What would I want to go sayin' a fool thing like that for?
PUD. Please, Gramps. Say it!
GRAMPS. (*With a look over his shoulder.*) Sinkpea.
PUD. Say it louder.
GRAMPS. Sinkpea! Sinkpea—sinkpea! (MARCIA *enters from* L. *arch. Crosses* R. C.)
MARCIA. (*Coming* L. *of table.*) What's that, Mr. Northrup?
GRAMPS. Sinkpea. . . . Oh, hello, Marcy. (MARCIA *crosses* D. R. PUD *kisses* GRAMPS. GRAMPS *puts* PUD *off his lap.*) There we are. Now, off to bed with you. Here you are, Marcy. 'Night, boy.
PUD. (*Wiping mouth.*) 'Night, Gramps. I'll see you early in the morning. (GRAMPS *rises.* MARCIA *picks up book from floor.*)
GRAMPS. Sleep tight. (*Doorbell off* U. R. *arch.*) I'll let Doctor Evans in, Marcy. (GRAMPS *off* U. *to* R. *arch.* MARCIA *and* PUD *follow* L. *below table off* U. *to* L. *of arch. Exit* L.)
PUD. (*Sleepily.*) Marcy, I bet I sleep like my top tonight.
MARCIA. Of course you will, darling.
PUD. I should have been in bed hours ago.
GRAMPS. (*Off-stage.*) Come right in. (GRAMPS *on. Crosses* R. C. EVANS *crosses* D. L. *Puts hat on sideboard, satchel* L. *below table.* GRIMES *holds* C.) Mr. Grimes. I'm glad to make your acquaintance.
GRIMES. Yeah.
GRAMPS. Well, set down, Evans. (EVANS *sits chair* L. GRIMES *chair* R. GRAMPS *holds above table.* GRIMES *leaves hat on.*) Set down, Mr. Grimes. Have a nip?
GRIMES. Haven't got time for that, Northrup. We've got to . . .
EVANS. As a matter of fact, Northrup, I've been telling Mr. Grimes about Mr. Brink and the tree.
GRAMPS. Now, what did you want to go doin' that for?
EVANS. Well, he's very interested.
GRAMPS. (*To* GRIMES.) Don't suppose you believe he's up there?
GRIMES. (*Chuckling.*) Sure, sure, I believe it. I was just going to ask you to come along with me and talk it over. (*Looks at* EVANS.)

Another fellow I'd like to have you meet who wants to hear about it.

GRAMPS. It's this way, Mr. Grimes, I don't want any more people knowin' about this thing until I find out some way of provin' it. This is goin' to be a hard thing to make people believe. 'Tain't everybody that can hear Mr. Brink when he talks. I figger that . . .

GRIMES. (*With look to* EVANS.) Oh, what the hell's the use? Now try to get this straight, will you? I'm taking you to the state insane asylum! (*Pause.* GRAMPS *is dazed.*)

GRAMPS. (*Softly.*) You're takin' me . . . ? You're takin' me to the insane . . . (*Rises. Looks at* EVANS, *who shifts uncomfortably.*) Demetria!

EVANS. It's this way, Northrup. . . .

GRAMPS. (*Softly.*) Demmie! . . . Where is Demmie, Evans?

EVANS. Well, she's . . .

GRAMPS. Where is she?

EVANS. Well, she's outside in the car.

GRAMPS. Waitin', eh? (GRAMPS *sits.*) Waitin' for Pud.

EVANS. It's just for observation, Northrup. And she'll just keep Pud until you get back.

GRIMES. Sure. Sure. Now, you come along with me and do as you're told and you may get better soon and can come home again.

GRAMPS. There ain't nothin' wrong with me, Mr. Grimes.

GRIMES. Then we'll find that out.

GRAMPS. Honest, there ain't nothin' wrong with me.

GRIMES. Now, are you coming along like a good fellow or do I have to put a strait-jacket on you? (EVANS *rises. Holds* L. *Pause. They watch him.*)

GRAMPS. (*Softly.*) Sort of looks like I gotta, don't it? (*Moves two steps* C., *then turns as if to go out.*) Now, I'll just go up and say good-bye to Pud.

GRIMES. (*Blocking his way.*) No, no, you'll see him tomorrow. They'll bring him up to the asylum. (EVANS *crosses* R. *to* R. *of* GRAMPS.)

EVANS. Better come along, Northrup.

GRAMPS. Yes, maybe it's just as well.

GRIMES. All right. Come on. Let's get goin'.

GRAMPS. Sure. Sure. I'm goin' to go right along with you. Gonna march right up to the bug-house and surprise 'em.

GRIMES. (EVANS *crosses* L.) That's the way—surprise 'em.
GRAMPS. I guess it will surprise 'em to see how easy I come along.
GRIMES. (*Back of table.*) Sure it will. That's a good idea.
GRAMPS. All right. Come on. (GRAMPS *crosses* U. C. EVANS, *crossing* L., *gets hat. Starts with* GRIMES.) Oh, wait!
GRIMES. What's the matter?
GRAMPS. My badge. I've got to have my badge like I wear in parades. I'm a veteran, you know.
GRIMES. Fine! You couldn't march without your badge, now could you?
GRAMPS. No, siree. (GRAMPS *crosses* R. *to desk. Fumbles in it.* EVANS *sits chair to pick up kit.* GRIMES *leans above him.* GRIMES *winks at* EVANS. EVANS *shakes his head.*)
GRIMES. It's all in knowing how to handle 'em. Sometimes the best way is to humor 'em; but sometimes you got to be tough with 'em.
GRAMPS. Here it is. Afraid for a minute it was upstairs. Now then. (GRAMPS *crosses* R. C., *holding gun in hand.* GRIMES *gives* L.)
EVANS. Put that down, Northrup!
GRIMES. Yeah, put it down now. Put it down.
GRAMPS. (*Points finger at them.*) Ah! Ah! You know you got to humor a crazy person. And since you've both made up your minds that I'm crazy you can understand it would drive me wild, if you didn't humor me.
EVANS. Be careful, Northrup. You're going to get yourself into trouble. This is no way of getting out of it.
GRAMPS. Only way that occurs to me at the minute. Now listen, I ain't goin' to no bug-house!
GRIMES. Listen, Northrup . . .
GRAMPS. I ain't goin' to no bug-house and I ain't goin' to let that old she-cat get Pud. But I see I gotta prove that what I been sayin' in reference to a certain Mr. Brink ain't no poppycock.
EVANS. Now be reasonable, Northrup.
GRIMES. Yeah, you can prove it to us later.
GRAMPS. Wait a minute. (*Slight pause.* GRAMPS' *eye lights on* EVANS' *satchel.*) That your medicine kit, Evans?
EVANS. Yes.
GRAMPS. What you got in that kit?
EVANS. Lots of things.
GRAMPS. You got anything in it—poison enough to kill a fly?
EVANS. Of course, but . . .

GRIMES. (*Advancing.*) You can play with all the flies you want when——

GRAMPS. Play! Do you consider it playin' when a man is willin' to risk his freedom on a fly?

EVANS. What's a fly got to do with it?

GRAMPS. I'll make a bargain with you. And you'd best take it, too, because if you don't I'm just liable to go wild as all hell. (*Wiggles gun at them.*)

GRIMES. Well, what's the bargain?

GRAMPS. You take the worst poison you got in that bag and put some of it in a tumbler. Then you catch a fly and put him in the poison. If that fly dies, I'll give myself up to you, to the police, to anyone, go to the insane asylum, do anythin' you say. (GRIMES *and* EVANS *look at each other.*) Well?

EVANS. If the fly dies, you'll come along with us without makin' any trouble?

GRAMPS. Yup. I promise. Hope to die. Cross my heart.

EVANS. Well—— (*Gives* C. *to* GRAMPS.)

GRAMPS. (*Pointing gun.*) It's the easiest way, Mr. Grimes.

GRIMES. (*With look to* EVANS.) All right.

EVANS. O. K.

GRAMPS. You get the poison. I'll get the glasses and—(*Pointing with gun.*) Mr. Grimes, you catch a fly. (GRAMPS *crosses* U. R. *to shelf.*)

GRIMES. He's crazy, raving crazy.

EVANS. Looks like it. But don't think he won't use that gun! I know the old boy. . . .

GRIMES. O. K. Let him play with the fly. How do we know he'll keep his word, though?

EVANS. I think he will.

GRIMES. The word of a nut——

EVANS. (*Sharply.*) Well, what do you want to do? Take the gun away from him?

GRIMES. (*Looking around at gun.*) No, no. Let him do it! No hurry. (GRAMPS *crosses* D. R. *Puts 2 glasses on table.*)

GRAMPS. Of course, look here, a bet ain't a bet that don't cut both ways. If the fly lives, you gotta swear I'm sane.

GRIMES. Well, I don't know.

EVANS. Don't worry. (GRAMPS *holds* R. C.) I know damn well I can kill a fly.

GRAMPS. No, you can't!

EVANS. If I can't kill a fly, I'll quit medicine. (*With look to* GRIMES.) You'll agree to this, won't you, Grimes?

GRIMES. Oh, all right.

GRAMPS. You swear?

EVANS. Yes, we swear, Northrup.

GRIMES. Sure, sure, that's all right. You don't have to worry about us.

GRAMPS. All right. Where's the fly? (GRAMPS *crosses* R. *to door. Catches fly in hand, crosses to table.*) Wait a minute. Here's one.

EVANS. Got him?

GRAMPS. Yeah. Now, take the tumbler, get the poison. (EVANS *takes poison and tweezers from his bag.*) Don't get so excited, little fly. You'll be buzzin' around just as good as new pretty soon.

GRIMES. You're the funniest one I've seen, Northrup. (*Laughs.*)

GRAMPS. Yup. Guess I am. (*Laughs.*)

EVANS. All right. (EVANS *pours poison in 1 tumbler.*) Here's enough poison to kill a horse. (GRAMPS *puts fly in empty glass.* EVANS *covers with hand, inverts glass over poison, taps fly down into poison, puts empty glass down.* EVANS *shoves glass across table. All lean to watch.*) And there's your fly!

GRAMPS. He ain't much of a swimmer, is he? Leave him there. Let him get his belly full before you take him out. Well, you been practicin' medicine thirty years, ain't you, Evans?

EVANS. About that.

GRAMPS. And you still think you can kill a fly, eh?

EVANS. (*Gently.*) I've always thought I could, Northrup.

GRAMPS. Well, well, you live and learn, Evans, you live and learn. (GRAMPS *chuckles.* GRIMES *chuckles.*)

EVANS. All right. He's had time enough. (EVANS *lifts fly out of poison with tweezers, puts on folded newspaper. All lean over table.*)

GRAMPS. Looks kinda sick, don't he?

GRIMES. If I ever saw anything deader I don't know what it is.

EVANS. He's dead, Northrup. (EVANS *sits chair* L. GRAMPS *stirs the fly. Pause. They watch it.*)

GRIMES. Don't tell us we don't know when something's dead.

GRAMPS. Wait a minute. Give this fly a chance. You can't come to yourself all of a sudden.

GRIMES. You're tough all right, Northrup. Tough but crazy. (*Pause. To* EVANS.) Well?

EVANS. He'll come along, I think.

GRIMES. Let's get going then. (*They look at* GRAMPS. *He seems bewildered and beaten but stares at fly.*)

EVANS. (*Crosses to* GRAMPS.) All right, Northrup. A bet's a bet.

GRAMPS. Well, I'll be damned. (*Sits* D. R. *Touches fly with gun.*)

EVANS. Come on now. Put down that gun. (EVANS *rises.* GRAMPS *rises sadly, turns to fly.*)

GRAMPS. Wait a minute . . . wait a minute—he moved. . . . (*Others look at paper, quickly.*)

EVANS. Huh?

GRAMPS. Look, look! (*All lean.*) He's drunk as a lord but we didn't say anythin' about that. He's movin' right across that damned piece of paper! (*All turn* U., *watching fly.*)

EVANS. I'll be damned! I'll be ——

GRIMES. Good God!

EVANS. What is this, Northrup? (EVANS *and* GRIMES *play* L. C. GRAMPS *holds* R.)

GRIMES. You didn't give him enough poison, Evans.

EVANS. I gave him enough poison to kill a million flies.

GRIMES. Something went wrong.

EVANS. You saw the fly in the poison yourself.

GRAMPS. Well, now will you believe what I've been tellin' you about Mr. Brink?

GRIMES. To hell with that! Put down that gun, Northrup. (GRIMES *crosses* C. *to* GRAMPS, *pulls out handcuffs above table.*)

GRAMPS. Hey, wait a minute, you said ——

GRIMES. Put it down now! I don't know what kind of a trick this is ——

EVANS. You promised him, Grimes. (EVANS *crosses* U. C. *to* GRIMES.)

GRIMES. I came to get him and, by God, I'm going to do it! What's a promise to a lunatic?

GRAMPS. So you don't believe it yet, eh? Even after I proved it to you?

GRIMES. (*Softly.*) You crazy bastard ——

EVANS. Look out, Grimes. Wait a minute! (EVANS *crosses* C. *to* R *of* GRAMPS.)

GRAMPS. And you ain't goin' to keep your word, eh? Well, by

God, there's another way of provin' it and it looks like I got to use that way right now.

EVANS. For God's sake, Northrup! What ——

GRAMPS. I'm goin' to make another experiment and I want you to witness it.

GRIMES. (*Going toward* EVANS.) He's crazy as hell! He's dangerous!

EVANS. What are you going to do, Northrup!

GRAMPS. Evans, at this close range if a man was shot right through the belly, he'd die, wouldn't he?

EVANS. Good God, man!

GRIMES. Look out there, Northrup!

GRAMPS. Wouldn't he?

EVANS. Yes, of course, but ——

GRAMPS. That's all I want to know. (GRAMPS *shoots* GRIMES, *who falls over chair* L. *to floor* D. C. *below table.* EVANS *stoops above him.*) Now, don't worry. He ain't goin' to die.

EVANS. You crazy fool! He'll be dead in an hour. (GRAMPS *crosses* R. *out door* R. *to corner* R. *end porch. Holds. Looks up at tree.*)

GRAMPS. Stay up there, Mr. Brink. If you come down now, by God, I'm in a hell of a fix.

CURTAIN

ACT II

SCENE 3

Dawn.

AT RISE: EVANS *is holding long fishpole over fence. He pulls it out, there is gray object on end of it. He kneels over it, studies it carefully with magnifying glass.* MARCIA *comes out porch when he examines mouse. Enter* MARCIA D. L. *door. Holds on porch.* EVANS' *kit on* R. *end porch. Sees* EVANS.

MARCIA. (*Startled.*) Oh. (EVANS *looks up with a start.*) Oh, good morning, Doctor Evans. I didn't know you were here.

EVANS. Good morning, Marcia.

MARCIA. Did you want to see Mr. Northrup?
EVANS. Why—why, yes, I did. Is he up yet?
MARCIA. Yes. He and Pud are just finishing breakfast. I'll tell him you're here. He'll be right out.
EVANS. Yes, yes, do that.
MARCIA. Is anything the matter? (MARCIA *crosses* C. *to* EVANS.)
EVANS. No—I've been up all night.
MARCIA. (*Pointing.*) Is that a mouse, Doctor Evans?
EVANS. Yes, Marcia, that's a mouse.
MARCIA. Oh. (MARCIA *off* D. L. *She looks at him wonderingly, goes in. Pause.* EVANS *examines mouse again, gets up.* EVANS *crosses* D. R. *below tree.*)
EVANS. Hello. (*Pause. No answer.*) Hello up there. (*Pause. No answer.* PILBEAM *enters* U. R. *Holds on* R. *end porch.*) Hello.
PILBEAM. Hello. (EVANS *turns sharply.*)
EVANS. (*Crosses* C.) Oh, hello, Pilbeam. I was just—er ——
PILBEAM. (*Crosses* C.) Feeling all right?
EVANS. Of course. Why?
PILBEAM. I just wondered—well—(PILBEAM *crosses* C. *to* L.) what do you want to see me about?
EVANS. Thought I might need you.
PILBEAM. Oh. (*Pause.* PILBEAM *watches* EVANS *curiously.*) Hear you didn't lock Northrup up last night.
EVANS. That's right.
PILBEAM. How's that?
EVANS. He isn't crazy.
PILBEAM. What? (PILBEAM *crosses* C. *to* EVANS.)
EVANS. (*Louder.*) He's not crazy. (*Crosses* R. C. *by tree. Picks up fishpole.*)
PILBEAM. Oh. (*Pause.*) What you got there?
EVANS. Fishpole.
PILBEAM. Going fishing? (PILBEAM *crosses to* L. *of* EVANS.)
EVANS. Been fishing.
PILBEAM. Catch much? Well, that's a mouse.
EVANS. Yeah. That's a mouse.
PILBEAM. Well, what the hell's the matter with you, Evans?
EVANS. What do you mean—what's the matter?
PILBEAM. You got me out of bed.
EVANS. Wait a minute, Pilbeam. Now, don't get excited. We got to keep our heads. Because something's happened that'll turn this

world upside-down, unless we can stop it. And you gotta help me.

PILBEAM. Uh?

EVANS. Northrup shot Grimes last night, Pilbeam.

PILBEAM. Good God!

EVANS. Shot him right through the belly. He had internal hemorrhages and it was an hour before I could get him to the hospital.

PILBEAM. What did he shoot him for?

EVANS. He was experimenting. (*Looks at tree.*)

PILBEAM. He was—experimenting! (*Looks at tree.*)

EVANS. Wait a minute. Grimes is all right.

PILBEAM. All right?

EVANS. He's practically well. (*Crosses* C. *Puts pole* U. *side on porch.*) That's the trouble. According to everything I know about medicine, Grimes should have died last night, Pilbeam. But he didn't. (*Wipes face.* EVANS *crosses to* L. *of* PILBEAM. *Sits* C. *edge porch.*) Plenty of things should have died last night. But they didn't. (*Pauses a second, continues in a confused voice.*) I've been up all night, trying to kill something. I've experimented on everything I could get my hands on. Insects. Bugs. I've tried to kill every stray cat or dog I could find. I couldn't kill a damned thing. Except that mouse. (PILBEAM *silent.* EVANS *rises.*) And do you know how I killed him? I tied him to the end of this fishpole and touched him to that tree.

PILBEAM. Look here, Evans, you've been up all night——

EVANS. Oh, for God's . . . (*Crosses* D. R.) Don't see anything up there, do you?

PILBEAM. Of course not. (*Crosses* D. R. C.)

EVANS. (*Crosses to* L. C.) Hear anything?

PILBEAM. Not a rustle.

EVANS. Neither do I. But if there is anything up there, by God, it's got to come down. It's got to come down. And you got to help me! (*Both look back at tree.* GRAMPS *enters* D. L. *door, holds porch. They whirl, startled.*)

GRAMPS. Howdy, Evans. Howdy, Pilbeam. (MARCIA *and* PUD U. C. *house, off* U. *to* L. *arch.*)

PILBEAM. Oh, hello, Northrup.

EVANS. Hello.

GRAMPS. How's Mr. Grimes doin'?

EVANS. Seems to be doing all right. (GRAMPS *sits* L. C. *porch.*)

GRAMPS. (*Chuckles.*) Glad to hear it. Nasty accident. Well, set down. What can I do for you? (*Pause.* EVANS *crosses to bench, sits.* PILBEAM *crosses to* R. *of* C.)

EVANS. Guess I owe you an apology, Northrup. (PILBEAM *holds* R. C.)

GRAMPS. No, you don't. Wouldn't have any respect for you if you believed a thing like this at first. You're a doctor . . .(*To* PILBEAM.) Kinda interestin', ain't it, Pilbeam?

PILBEAM. Why—er—of course—very interesting.

GRAMPS. Awful nice sort of chap, Mr. Brink is. Real friendly.

BRINK. Thank you very much.

GRAMPS. (*Rises.*) Oh, mornin', Mr. Brink. Didn't know you were up yet. (EVANS *rises, looks at* GRAMPS, *the tree, then sits.* PILBEAM *looks at* GRAMPS, *then at tree.*)

BRINK. Oh, yes. I've had a lovely morning. I've had a mouse in my face.

GRAMPS. (*Looks at* EVANS.) What! (*Rises, crosses* C.) Gol-darn it, what you been up to, Evans? Have you been shovin' a mouse in my friend Brink's face?

PILBEAM. (PILBEAM *crosses* D. R. C. *to* GRAMPS.) Good God, how do you know that?

GRAMPS. Mr. Brink told me, just now.

PILBEAM. I've got to go! (PUD *scrambles* R. *end porch.* EVANS *crosses* U. R. C. *to* PILBEAM, *holds him back.*)

EVANS. Wait a minute, Pilbeam. (PILBEAM *hesitates.*)

PILBEAM. I've got a busy day, Jim. I got a lot of work to do ——

EVANS. Stick around, Pilbeam. (GRAMPS *sits* L. C. *porch.* EVANS *crosses* D. R. C. PILBEAM *holds* R. *end porch.*)

GRAMPS. Sure, stick around. This is a sort of special occasion. In fact, this is the mornin' Demmie figured I'd be in the nut-house. Yes, sir, I'm feelin' right good this mornin'. Pud's feelin' pretty spry. Mr. Brink sounded pretty pert. Everybody's feelin' fine—'cept Demmie. God bless her!

EVANS. Northrup? (*Crosses* C. *Sits* R. *of* GRAMPS.)

GRAMPS. Yeah.

EVANS. There's a man in my hospital who's been suffering for ten years. He's in constant pain.

GRAMPS. I'm real sorry, Evans.

EVANS. Day before yesterday, I decided to operate on him. The operation wasn't successful. He's in more pain now than he ever was.

GRAMPS. Well, Evans, I'm real sorry to hear that.

EVANS. I expected him to die last night. I hoped he would.

GRAMPS. Yeah.

EVANS. There's a nice old lady up in 2C, Mrs. Trenner, remember her?

GRAMPS. The old lady who used to have all the dogs?

EVANS. Yeah.

GRAMPS. By God, I'd forgot all about her.

EVANS. Everybody has. She's been in there for six years, in bed. She hasn't got much left. Only one idea—to die. And this is what's happening in just one small hospital, you know. In a small town. There are two in Gainesville. There are several million in the world, aren't there—full of people just like that.

GRAMPS. I'm sorry for all those people—sorry for all of 'em—but if you're hintin' for me to let Mr. Brink down, you're off on the wrong track. (EVANS *looks at* GRAMPS *a moment.*)

EVANS. What do you think is going to happen, Northrup, in the next few days when people find out there's no more death?

PILBEAM. But it isn't true ——

EVANS. (*Crosses to* PILBEAM.) No more death. Think about it for a minute. Nobody died last night. Nobody's going to die tonight. Or tomorrow night. Nobody's going to die . . . (*Looks at* GRAMPS.) . . . until Northrup says they can. What do you think about that?

PILBEAM. It's absurd.

EVANS. That's right. It's absurd. (*Facing* GRAMPS.) Five years from today this world will be so overcrowded that it won't be fit to live in . . . think of the disease . . .

GRAMPS. I don't give a damn! I don't care what happens! I've got Mr. Brink up there and he's gonna stay there!

EVANS. (*Crosses to bench.*) He can't, Northrup. You gotta let him down.

GRAMPS. Why should I? I'm lookin' after Pud and myself.

EVANS. Who the hell are you?

GRAMPS. I'm the feller that got Mr. Brink up that tree and up that tree he's gonna stay until I'm good and ready to let him down.

PILBEAM. (*Frightened.*) Well, I've got to get back to the office. I've got work to do. I've got a hell of a lot of work to do today. 'Bye, Northrup. (*No answer.*) Good-bye, Evans. (*No answer. Looks at tree.*) Good-b —— (PILBEAM *off* U. R.)

GRAMPS. Look here, Evans, 'tain't that I'm afraid to go. I ain't afraid of dyin'. Might be real pleasant to see what's comin' next. But, you see, there's Pud. I just want to stick around in case he needs me. (*Pause.*)

EVANS. Have you ever seen a man a hundred and ten years old, Northrup?

GRAMPS. Yep. I seen one pretty near that old once. Old Fred Brown's father. Poor old devil —— Hey, what the hell are you drivin' at?

EVANS. I was just thinking—by the time Pud's a young man, you'll be getting about that age yourself.

GRAMPS. No. No. When I saw myself gettin' like that old guy was I'd let Mr. Brink come down and take me.

EVANS. Oh, no, you wouldn't.

GRAMPS. Yes, I would.

EVANS. You wouldn't be able to see yourself getting like that. You'd be too far gone by that time. You might even forget Mr. Brink was up there. (*Pause.* GRAMPS *sits thinking.*) You gotta let him down, Northrup. (*Pause.*)

GRAMPS. (*Softly.*) I don't want to be no nuisance to Pud ——

EVANS. You've got to let Mr. Brink come down today. I warn you —I'll do everything I can to make you. Better think it over. (EVANS *picks up kit, turns to* GRAMPS.) I'll be back in an hour. (*Starts out, then hesitates.*) Well, thanks for not letting me eat that apple yesterday.

GRAMPS. You kin have one now, if you want it.

EVANS. No, thanks. Well—good-bye, Northrup.

GRAMPS. Good-bye.

EVANS. I'm—I'm sorry. (EVANS *off* U. C. R. *Carries kit and hat.*)

GRAMPS. Yeah. Mr. Brink, if I let you come down, you're bound and determined you're gonna take me, ain't you?

BRINK. You will be the first.

GRAMPS. That's what I thought. . . . No way of getting out of that, is there?

BRINK. None.

GRAMPS. No, I didn't think so.

BRINK. It would seem to me that you had got out of a great deal already.

GRAMPS. I just wondered. I just wondered. Don't get upset. (*Crosses* R. C. *to tree.*) Mr. Brink, do you think Evans is right

about me and Pud? Think maybe I might become a nuisance to the boy?
BRINK. My dear man, there's no doubt about it.
GRAMPS. H'mmn. (*Crosses* C. *Sits porch.*)
PUD. (*Enters* U. C. R. *Crosses* D. R. C. *Holds* R. *end of porch.*) Here comes Casey down the track . . . bingety, bingety, bing. . . . Here comes Casey down the track . . . bingety, bingety, bing . . . Choo, choo, choo . . . (*Across stage to down* R.) Choo, choo, choo. . . . (*Stops.*) Say, God, you are standing there in the middle of my track. Get out of the way, God; get off my railroad track or I'll run over you. . . . I guess I'll have to strike you dead, Casey. . . . BOOM! . . . Now, look what you did, God, you wrecked my train all to splinters. Now I have to get a new engine. . . . All right, Casey, here's a new engine. . . . Thanks, God. Get on and I'll give you a ride. Here we go . . . choo, choo, choo . . . ding, ding. . . . Get out of the way, everybody. Get out of the way. Here comes God and Casey Jones. . . . Toot, toot! Toot. (PUD *plays to* C. *Bumps* GRAMPS. *Hugs him.*) Toot, choo, choo. . . . I love you, Gramps, I love you more'n my engine!

CURTAIN

ACT II

SCENE 4

Toward close of same day.

AT RISE: SHERIFF *is reading.* EVANS *seated on horse* R. (*Has no kit in scene.*) GRAMPS *sits* C., *with* PUD *to his* R. SHERIFF BURLINGHAME, DEMETRIA *and* EVANS *are from* L. *to* R. MARCIA *is just coming out on porch, stands* L.

SHERIFF. ". . . signed, James Evans, M. D."
GRAMPS. Just read the last part of that document again, Sheriff. Where Doctor Evans signed. . . .
SHERIFF. All right, Northrup. " Dr. James Evans, having testified that the said Julian Northrup is incapable of managing himself and his property, it is the order of this Court that he be com-

mitted to the Gainesville Institution for the Insane, according to the Laws of this State and it is further ordered that the custody of the child, John Gilford Northrup, be awarded to his aunt, Demetria Riffle."

GRAMPS. Thank you, Sheriff. (*Turns to* EVANS.) You've kinda fixed me up good and proper, ain't you?

EVANS. I warned you I'd do anything I could.

GRAMPS. (*To* SHERIFF.) So, Evans has told you I'm crazy, ain't he?

SHERIFF. I guess there's no doubt about that, Northrup.

DEMETRIA. (*Crosses to* C.) I'll be good to the boy while you're in the asylum, Julian. I really will. . . . (DEMETRIA *crosses* C. *to* PUD. PUD *crosses to* L. *of* GRAMPS.) Come, Pud, you're to come home with me now.

PUD. (*Clutching* GRAMPS.) Gramps!

SHERIFF. Come along, Northrup.

GRAMPS. Wait a minute. (*They all stop.*) I'd like to speak to Pud a minute first. (EVANS *and* SHERIFF *look at each other.*)

EVANS. You two wait out in the car a moment. (DEMETRIA, *followed by* SHERIFF, *crosses off* R. *via porch.* EVANS *holds* R. C.) I'm sorry, Northrup, but I've given you all day to make up your mind. I can't wait any longer. So you're going to the insane asylum.

GRAMPS. You're pretty smart, ain't you, Evans? You figger I won't go to the nut-house. You figger I'll let Mr. Brink down instead.

EVANS. I'm hoping you will.

GRAMPS. You figger long as I lost the boy, I don't much care what happens to me.

EVANS. That's what I figure, Northrup.

GRAMPS. All right. You're a pretty smart feller. (EVANS *off porch* R. PUD *crosses* R. *end porch after* EVANS *holds.*)

PUD. What's the matter with Doctor Evans, Gramps?

GRAMPS. Guess he's kinda sorry, boy. (*Crosses to front of bench, sits* R.)

PUD. What's he sorry for?

GRAMPS. (MARCIA *crosses upstage.*) Come here a minute.

PUD. O. K. (PUD *crosses to* GRAMPS. *Sits porch* R. *of* GRAMPS.)

GRAMPS. I'm goin' away, boy.

PUD. Where, Gramps?

GRAMPS. Where the woodbine twineth.

PUD. You goin' with Mr. Brink?

GRAMPS. Yep, I'm goin' with Mr. Brink. You see, your Gramps is gettin' to be a pretty old man. And when you get to be a pretty old man you begin to get kinda tired.

PUD. Are you tired?

GRAMPS. Right at this minute, I'm pretty dog-gone tired.

PUD. Let's lie down and rest.

GRAMPS. That's just what I'm gonna do. But the only way an old man can really lie down and rest is to go with Mr. Brink.

PUD. I'll go with you, Gramps.

GRAMPS. No, you can't go with me, boy. You've got your whole life ahead of you.

PUD. Don't want my whole life ahead of me. I want to go with you. I love you, Gramps. (*Puts arms around* GRAMPS.)

GRAMPS. Shouldn't love me that much, boy. You see, Pud, I been thinkin' things over. Maybe it ain't such a good thing for you to be livin' with me any more. And, you know, maybe your Aunt Demetria (PUD *rises.*) ain't as much of a pismire as we thought she was. (PUD *turns* R. *away from* GRAMPS.)

PUD. Gramps!

GRAMPS. No, sir, maybe she ain't. Maybe it'd be better if you was to go over to your Aunt Demetria's house and live with her. (PUD *backs further away.*) What's the matter, boy?

PUD. Don't you love me any more, Gramps?

GRAMPS. Pshaw, boy, I'm just tryin' to make you understand——

PUD. Gramps, you don't love me any more.

GRAMPS. Of course I do. It's just that I gotta go away. (PUD *crosses to* GRAMPS. *Leans on him,* R. *of him.*)

PUD. But I'll go with you, Gramps.

GRAMPS. But you can't, boy, you can't.

PUD. Please, Gramps, please!

GRAMPS. No.

PUD. (*Gives* R.) Then I don't love you any more either. . . . I don't love you any more either. . . . (*Turns and runs off* U. C. R., *crying.*)

GRAMPS. Wait a minute, boy, wait a minute.

BRINK. That's the better way.

GRAMPS. Maybe so.

BRINK. He will forget.

GRAMPS. Maybe so. (EVANS, SHERIFF, DEMETRIA *on* R. *cross* C. *on porch. Hold.*)
SHERIFF. What about it, Northrup?
GRAMPS. Oh, I ain't goin' with you. I'm goin' with Mr. Brink. Didn't Evans tell you about Mr. Brink?
SHERIFF. Oh, yeah. He did. Well, get it over with. We haven't got all night.
EVANS. Take it easy, Sheriff. . . . Northrup, would you rather we left you alone? (MARCIA *on* D. L. EVANS *crosses* L. *of* GRAMPS.)
GRAMPS. No. As a matter of fact, I'd like to have somebody around. (DEMETRIA *crosses* C. *to* R. *of* GRAMPS.)
DEMETRIA. (*Going to him.*) Well, Julian . . .
GRAMPS. Demmie, honest to God, will you be good to Pud?
DEMETRIA. I'll be good to him, Julian.
GRAMPS. Will you see he gets some fun out of life?
DEMETRIA. I will.
GRAMPS. Will you not keep huggin' him all the time like you do?
DEMETRIA. I'll be good to Pud, Julian. You don't have to worry. I have wonderful plans for him already.
GRAMPS. What plans you got for him?
DEMETRIA. Well, I'm going to start right in getting him ready to go to school next year.
GRAMPS. How d'ye mean, gettin' him ready?
DEMETRIA. I'm gonna start teaching him things myself, Julian. So that when he gets to school, he'll be way ahead of any of the others.
GRAMPS. Ain't you gonna let him play any?
DEMETRIA. Of course, Julian. He'll have his play period. But now he'll have education too. I'll begin to form his mind. . . .
GRAMPS. His mind's formin' all right as it is.
DEMETRIA. And I'll teach him little poems to recite.
GRAMPS. Oh, my God!
DEMETRIA. I'll teach him how to behave nicely, Julian. How to say "Yes, sir" and "No, sir" and how to curtsey when older people——
GRAMPS. Curtsey! Pud!
DEMETRIA. And by the time Miss Ramsdell's school opens in the Fall . . .
GRAMPS. Miss Ramsdell's school is a girls' school!

DEMETRIA. Not any more, Julian. They're going to have three little boys in it next year.

GRAMPS. You're gonna make Pud into a sissy! (*Rises. Crosses* D. C.) By God, you are still a pismire! I'm gonna change my mind. I ain't goin' with Mr. Brink. I'm gonna stay right here and take care of Pud. (GRAMPS *sits.* DEMETRIA *gives* L. *to* EVANS.)

EVANS. (*Sharply.*) Northrup! How can you take care of Pud if you're in the asylum?

GRAMPS. Oh.

EVANS. Because that's where you'll be.

GRAMPS. Yeah. Well, what the hell am I gonna do? (*Slight pause.*) Well, no use stretchin' it out. (GRAMPS *gets bright idea! Rises.*) 'Bye, Marcy.

MARCIA. Oh, Mr. Northrup. (MARCIA *gives* L.)

EVANS. (*Crossing to* GRAMPS.) I realize what I'm asking you to do, Northrup.

GRAMPS. Yeah. . . . (EVANS *crosses* C. *to* C. *and* R. GRAMPS *crosses* R. C. *to tree.*) Well, Mr. Brink, looks kinda like the time has come. (GRAMPS *crosses* R. C.)

BRINK. Yes, the time has come now.

GRAMPS. I expect you're all ready.

BRINK. All ready as soon as you say the word.

GRAMPS. I hope you ain't goin' to hold nothin' against me, Mr. Brink.

BRINK. We'll see. We'll see.

GRAMPS. Remember the only reason I got you up there was to keep Demmie from gettin' the boy.

BRINK. I've taken that into consideration.

GRAMPS. I wasn't cheatin'. I was gonna let you down as soon as you had word you was to take her.

BRINK. I know. I know. (DEMETRIA *clucks. Gives* L. *to* EVANS.)

GRAMPS. (*Looking at* DEMETRIA.) Don't suppose by any chance you've had any word about takin' her yet.

BRINK. No, there's been no call for Miss Riffle. There probably won't be for years.

GRAMPS. (*Suddenly.*) What's that? You say you were supposed to take her an hour ago?

BRINK. No, no. I said I probably wouldn't take her for years.

GRAMPS. My God, why didn't you tell me, Mr. Brink? Why, if you're supposed to take Demmie too ——

BRINK. But I am *not* supposed to take her!

EVANS. (*Crosses* C. *to* GRAMPS.) Northrup, did he really say that?

GRAMPS. Yep. Says he was supposed to take Demmie an hour ago. This changes everything. Come on, Demmie! (GRAMPS *crosses* L. C. *to* DEMETRIA. *Drags her* C. *She breaks away.* SHERIFF *holds* C. *porch.* MARCIA *holds* L. *porch.*)

DEMETRIA. No—no, Julian. This is absurd! This is —— Doctor Evans!

EVANS. I'm sorry, Miss Riffle. But when a person's time comes . . .

DEMETRIA. But—there isn't really anyone up in that tree —— This is all so—so silly.

GRAMPS. Thank you, Mr. Brink, for takin' Demmie. I wonder if you'd do one more thing. I wonder if after you've taken Demmie, you'd just slip the Sheriff in for good measure.

SHERIFF. Hey—what th' hell ——

GRAMPS. The old stiff's tryin' to take me to the nut-house ——

EVANS. Good God, Northrup! Do you know what you're doing? This is practically murder!

DEMETRIA. (*To* L. *of* EVANS.) M-m-murder! D-d-doctor! M-m-murder!

EVANS. Listen, you, all of you, Northrup's as sane as any one here.

SHERIFF. What's that? Hey, what is this, anyway?

EVANS. Northrup's not insane. You realize what he's going to do? Death is up in that tree. Northrup's talking to him. If he lets him down you're as good as dead, both of you.

DEMETRIA. What! What? I don't believe it ——

BRINK. This is ——

GRAMPS. (*To tree.*) Ssh! Ssh!

BRINK. This is the wildest absurdity I ever heard. You know perfectly well I have no authorization to take any of these people. It is utterly out of the question.

GRAMPS. What's that? You say you'll take the Sheriff too? Thank you, Mr. Brink. I appreciate that a great deal.

DEMETRIA. (*Hysterically.*) I don't believe it ——! You can't frighten me! I didn't hear anything up in that tree! I didn't hear a blessed thing!

MARCIA. I did! I heard him!

GRAMPS. Eh? What's that?

MARCIA. I heard him! (MARCIA *crosses* R. C. *to* GRAMPS.) I heard Mr. Brink!

GRAMPS. You did —— Now look here, Marcy!

DEMETRIA. You d-didn't ——

MARCIA. I did! I did! I heard him just as plain as I hear you. (DEMETRIA *looks at* EVANS.)

GRAMPS. But, Marcy ——

MARCIA. (*Quiets him with gesture.*) And he said that if he could just come down he would take anyone Mr. Northrup asked him to. (GRAMPS *holds his hands.*)

DEMETRIA. He didn't! He didn't say he was going to take me?

MARCIA. Oh, yes, he did, Miss Riffle. He said he was going to take you—first! (DEMETRIA *sits on bench.*)

BRINK. That girl ——

GRAMPS. Ssh! Ssh!

BRINK. That girl cannot hear a word I say. She is the most inordinate liar I ever met.

GRAMPS. Hear him then, Marcy?

MARCIA. Yes.

GRAMPS. What did he say? Now, be careful.

MARCIA. He said to please hurry and let him down. He's getting nervous and can't stand it another minute.

GRAMPS. Yup. That's just what he said. So I better get started. Don't want to make him any angrier.

BRINK. That would be impossible. You let me down!

GRAMPS. Well, good-bye, everybody. But then I'll be seein' you two in a second. Now I'm gonna start the magic words. (*Takes* DEMETRIA *and* SHERIFF *by hand.*) Come on, Demmie. Sheriff. Line up. Here we go. Off to glory! (GRAMPS *crosses* L. C. *to* DEMETRIA. *Takes her on his* L., *grabs* SHERIFF R. *and crosses* R. C. *to tree. General hubbub. He starts mumbling.*)

BRINK. (*Ad lib.*) Stop that monkey-business and let me down.

EVANS. (*Ad lib.*) Stop it, Northrup!

DEMETRIA. (*Ad lib.*) Stop him! Stop him, somebody! Stop him.

SHERIFF. (*Ad lib.*) Hold on there, Northrup. Hold on!

EVANS. (*Ad lib. Grabbing* GRAMPS.) Stop it, Northrup! Stop it! We'll do anything you want us to.

SHERIFF. (SHERIFF *gives* U. R. C. *to* GRAMPS, *tears paper.* EVANS *crosses* D. R. *to* SHERIFF.) Look, Northrup, look.

GRAMPS. All right! . . . (*Crosses* C. *to* DEMETRIA.) Now, you keep your hands off my boy, Demmie.

DEMETRIA. I will, Julian, I will.

GRAMPS. And you keep the hell away from me, too.
DEMETRIA. I will, Julian. I'll keep the hell away from you, too. (*Crosses* U. *to porch. Crosses* R. *and off* R.)
GRAMPS. All right. Mr. Brink, from now on, anybody who tries to make me let you down you gotta take them, too.
BRINK. I will not! I will not!
GRAMPS. Thank you very much. . . . (GRAMPS *gives* R. C. *to* EVANS *and* SHERIFF.) Now, you get out of here. All of you. I'm gonna stay right here and take care of Pud. I don't care if the whole damn world goes to hell. Git out of here. Git off my property. Go on. Go on! If you ask me, you got off pretty lucky. (EVANS *and* SHERIFF *off* D. R. GRAMPS *crosses* C. *to* MARCIA. MARCIA *crosses* C. *They sit* C. *porch.* GRAMPS R. *of* MARCIA.) Marcy, I love yuh. By God, I love yuh. And there ain't nothin' in this world can stop us now. Just you and me and Pud. Nothin' in the world can stop us, now.
BRINK. (*Appears.*) Which world do you mean?
GRAMPS. What's that, Mr. Brink?
BRINK. Which world do you mean?
GRAMPS. Why—I don't understand, Mr. Brink.
BRINK. Of course you don't. My poor man!
MARCIA. What did he say, Mr. Northrup?
GRAMPS. He said: "My poor man." And I didn't like the way he said it, Marcy. I didn't like the way he said it.

CURTAIN

ACT II

SCENE 5

Few minutes later. It is dark.

BRINK *in tree.* MARCIA U. L. *in arch, calling off* U. L. *Enter* GRAMPS D. R. *Enter* PUD D. L.

GRAMPS. (*Off* D. R.) Pud! Pud!
MARCIA. (*Off* U. L.) Where are you, Pud? (GRAMPS *on* D. R. *crosses* R. C. MARCIA *on* U. *from* L. *arch, crosses* D. L. *in house. Out door* R. *Crosses* D. R. *to* GRAMPS—MARCIA *looks off* D. R.)

GRAMPS. We got to find him, Marcy. We got to find him. I got to explain to him.—Hey, boy, where are you?
MARCIA. Pud!
GRAMPS. You didn't see nothin' of him at all?
MARCIA. Not a thing. Maybe he went over to see Jimmy.
GRAMPS. You run over and see, Marcy. Don't think he'd stay over there this late. You go on.
MARCIA. I'll be right back, Mr. Northrup. (MARCIA *off* U. C. R. GRAMPS *crosses* U. *to porch. Crosses* R. *on porch off* R.)
GRAMPS. Pud! Hey, Pud! Where are you, boy? Time to come home now. Hey, boy, where are you? Pud! Pud! (PUD *on* D. L. *door.* PUD *crosses* C., *puts cap and bundle* R. *end porch. Sits.* BRINK *leans low in tree to* PUD.)
BRINK. Pud!
PUD. (*Tearfully.*) Hello there, Mr. Brink.
BRINK. What's the matter, Pud?
PUD. My Gramps doesn't love me any more.
BRINK. He doesn't?
PUD. No. Didn't you follow the conversation?
BRINK. Yes, what are you going to do, Pud?
PUD. I'm going to run away. Then he'll be sorry.
BRINK. What have you got there?
PUD. (*Showing them.*) These are some cookies I got. . . . And this is my watch fob Gramps wrote on for me. . . . And a couple of specimens.
BRINK. And you're really going to run away?
PUD. 'Course I am.
BRINK. I wouldn't if I were you.
PUD. You would too.
BRINK. They'll only find you and bring you back. You're not big enough to run away, my little man.
PUD. I am so! And I'm not your little man! I'm not a little man at all. I'll spit in your eye.
BRINK. You might find that difficult.
PUD. Why?
BRINK. I'm afraid you couldn't reach me.
PUD. I could too.
BRINK. You would be afraid.
PUD. I'm not afraid of the biggest giant on earth.
BRINK. How do you know I'm not the biggest giant on earth?

PUD. Because you're in the littlest tree.

BRINK. There is a certain logic in that. Your mind is taking shape. That's too bad that has to happen.

PUD. Why?

BRINK. Because man's logic is the most pitiful thing about him. It stands in his way. It confuses him, so that he can't quite see the giants. You won't be able to see them much longer.

PUD. Aw, I will too.

BRINK. No, you will not. Not until you are as old as your grandfather. Then you will be able to see them again.

PUD. Nuts. (PUD *rises, crosses* R. C. *to tree.*)

BRINK. You're not very polite.

PUD. I'm politer than you, you big squashapussoshapuss.

BRINK. I'm afraid I never heard that word before.

PUD. Neither did I.

BRINK. You can make up words?

PUD. Sure, I can do anything.

BRINK. No, you can't. You can't even climb a tree.

PUD. I can too. I climbed that tree before you got up it and I climbed down again. That's more than you can do.

BRINK. You're right about that. But you couldn't do it now. Why, you can't even climb that fence.

PUD. I could do it with one hand.

BRINK. Let's see you.

PUD. (D. R.) All right. (*Crosses* D. R. *Climbs on horse, grabs fence with* R. *hand.*)

BRINK. You'll never get up on that side. Better come over to this side. It's much easier.

PUD. Ouch, that hurts my hand. Guess I'll have to get myself a heap o' tape. (*Crosses* L. *to door* L.)

BRINK. Baby calf! Baby calf!

PUD. Who's a baby calf! (*Crosses* R. *end porch. Puts* R. *foot on batten by post. Swings* L. *foot to ledge on post. Holds branch, swings to fence above tree. Sits there.*)

BRINK. That's right. I never thought you could do it. I guess you must be stronger than I thought. Come on now. Just a little more. *Go along the edge there.* Get one leg over. There! That's it. Now you're here. Splendid! I guess you can do everything.

PUD. Golly, I can see far up here.

BRINK Can you see me now?

PUD. Yes. Gee, why do you make your voice so whispery, Mr. Brink?

BRINK. Don't you like it?

PUD. Yes.

BRINK. Good. Can you see me?

PUD. Yes, I can see you.

BRINK. Look at me!

PUD. Gee, you've got funny eyes, Mr. Brink. They make me dizzy. You've got ghost eyes. (*Slowly* PUD *stands up, gripping post.*)

BRINK. Look at me again. (PUD *does so.*) That's right. Keep on looking at me. Give me your hand. (PUD *leans* R. *to* BRINK, *hand out.*) Lean forward. (PUD *falls, then screams, calls.*)

PUD. (*In terror.*) Gramps! Gramps! Gramps!

CURTAIN

ACT II

SCENE 6

Later that night. Moonlight.

AT RISE: GRAMPS *is holding* PUD *in his arms.* GRAMPS *and* PUD C. *porch.* BRINK *is visible.*

PUD. Gramps, I want a heap o' tape, my back hurts, my back.

GRAMPS. Hush, boy, hush for a minute. . . . Mr. Brink.

BRINK. Yes?

GRAMPS. Pud's in terrible pain. Doctor Evans just left and says he'll never be able to walk again. Why did you let him do it, Mr. Brink?

BRINK. My dear man, I didn't mean to hurt the boy. I just meant to take him. It was the only way out. I even waited a day to let the others force you. But you were too clever for them.

GRAMPS. But you could have found some other way than to pick on the boy.

BRINK. It is only through the boy that I have any hope of getting down from here. He is the only reason that you won't let me come down. What if I should tell you that I'm bound to stay out the time to which you sentenced me? Until Miss Riffle dies?

GRAMPS. You're not, are you? You're not. You don't have to stay up there, do you?
BRINK. No. But I want you to understand how much it means to you, to your whole world, to deny me. Already the world is beginning to feel the pain and sorrow and bewilderment in keeping me here. It is getting worse every hour.
GRAMPS. I guess I tried to bite off more'n I could chew.
BRINK. Much more.
GRAMPS. Will you come down, please, and take us both?
BRINK. Gladly.
GRAMPS. Please come then. (BRINK *climbs down—up side tree—crosses* D. R. C. *to* GRAMPS R. *of him.*) Quickly.
PUD. Gramps—— (*Rises, carries* PUD C. *to* BRINK.)
GRAMPS. Yes, boy.
PUD. A heap o' tape. My back hurts so awful——
GRAMPS. Yes, boy. There, there, boy. Just a minute—just a minute. (*Lifts* PUD *to* BRINK.)
BRINK. No, you are first. Ah, that's better, isn't it?
GRAMPS. Well, well. He was quite a load before. He's light as a feather now. Here, here. (BRINK *touches* PUD, *then slowly* PUD *stands erect below* GRAMPS, C.)
PUD. (*Rousing.*) Hello, Mr. Brink.
BRINK. Hello, Pud.
PUD. Are we deaded, Gramps?
GRAMPS. Must be. I feel like a two-year-old. How do you feel?
PUD. I feel like a two-year-old, too, Gramps.
GRAMPS. Mr. Brink, why didn't you tell me it was goin' to be like this?
BRINK. My dear man, I've been trying to tell you how pleasant it is to go with me, but you wouldn't listen.
PUD. You talk so funny, Mr. Brink.
BRINK. Well, never mind me—come on. Come along! (BRINK *gives* U. R.)
PUD. But, where we goin', Gramps?
GRAMPS. (*Stops.*) Oh, yes—by golly, that's important. Where are we goin', Mr. Brink?
BRINK. You'll find out.
PUD. (*Looks at* BRINK.) How long will we be there?
BRINK. For eternity.
PUD. (*Looks at* GRAMPS.) How long is eternity, Gramps?

GRAMPS. Right smart piece of time, boy.
PUD. Anyway, we'll be there together, won't we, Gramps?
GRAMPS. You're damn right we will be! You're damn right!
GRANNY. (*Off stage.*) Juleyun! Juleyun, do you have to use such language in front of the boy? (*All look up.*)
GRAMPS. Oh, hell, I thought you said she'd changed! (BRINK, *followed by* GRAMPS, *leads* PUD *off* U. R. C. *as*)

CURTAIN

CONSTRUCTION OF THE APPLE TREE

The tree is built up on an armature, such as a sculptor uses in making a clay figure. The armature will control the over all dimensions in all directions, i. e., height, width, and thickness.

Great care should be taken in the construction of the armature as it must support the weight of all who climb into the tree, and it is a very difficult task to reinforce it after the skin has been put on.

Chicken wire of about a 1¼ inch mesh is stretched and stapled to cover the entire armature, being fastened to all the discs.

A papier-mâché made of a thin glue size and 4 inch by 2 inch strips of newspaper is then applied. The strips being placed individually and flat, so as to criss cross and overlap continually until the wire is completely covered. This procedure is repeated about five or six times allowing each layer to dry thoroughly before applying the next. Any cracks which appear from time to time will be covered by the succeeding layers of mâché. The final layer of mâché should be of strips of dark brown burlap, which when dry brushed approximates apple tree bark in texture and color.

The leaves are best made by cutting strips of muslin about 2 inches wide, paint on both sides with leaf green scene paint and allow to dry. Accordion fold the strip in about 5 inch pleats and run through the band saw in the shape of an apple leaf. Thread each leaf onto a piece of florist's wire and fasten to real twigs and branches applied to the tree.

The fruit problem is best handled by using real apples, picked for color, each threaded onto a piece of florist's wire and dipped into melted canning wax, to delay the inevitable rotting action.

LIST OF PROPERTIES

Engraving instruments
Watch fob
Small stones (a few)
Small bone
Frog
Small whisky bottle
Water glasses
Mourning handkerchief (lady's)
Pen and ink
Book
Knitting materials
Tatting materials
Glass with soda water in it
Tea-tray with tea things
Stick for Gramps
3 apples
Mixing bowl
Pipe and matches
Satchel
Spade
Newspaper
Revolver (with blank cartridge)
2 glasses
Tweezers
Handcuffs
Fishpole
Artificial mouse
Magnifying glass
Legal document
Bundle and cap
Cookies

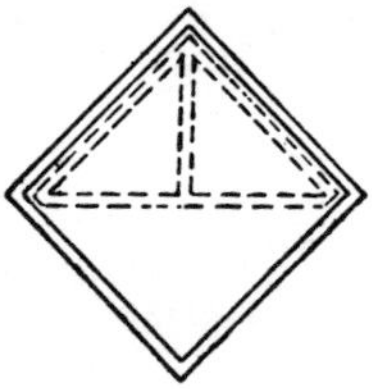

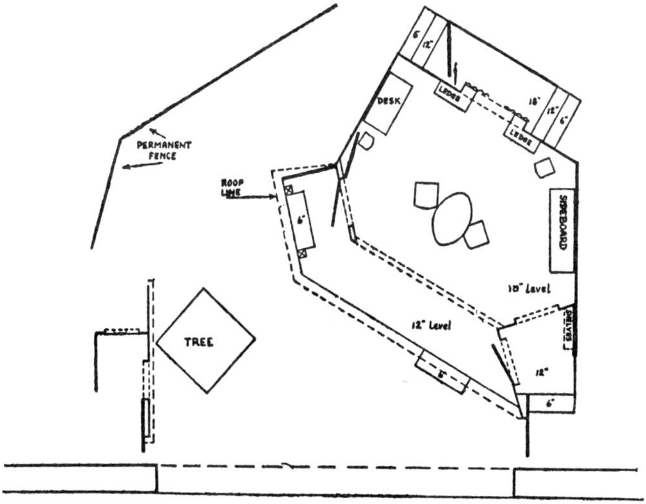
PERMANENT
FENCE
ROOF
LINE
DESK
LEDGE
LEDGE
SIDEBOARD
TREE
12" Level
SHELVES

TODAY'S HOTTEST NEW PLAYS

❑ **THREE VIEWINGS by Jeffrey Hatcher.** Three comic-dramatic monologues, set in a midwestern funeral parlor, interweave as they explore the ways we grieve, remember, and move on. *"Finally, what we have been waiting for: a new, true, idiosyncratic voice in the theater. And don't tell me you hate monologues; you can't hate them more than I do. But these are much more: windows into the deep of each speaker's fascinating, paradoxical, unique soul, and windows out into a gallery of surrounding people, into hilarious and horrific coincidences and conjunctions, into the whole dirty but irresistible business of living in this damnable but spellbinding place we presume to call the world." - New York Magazine.* [1M, 2W]

❑ **HAVING OUR SAY by Emily Mann.** The Delany Sisters' Bestselling Memoir is now one of Broadway's Best-Loved Plays! Having lived over one hundred years apiece, Bessie and Sadie Delany have plenty to say, and their story is not simply African-American history or women's history...it is our history as a nation. *"The most provocative and entertaining family play to reach Broadway in a long time." - New York Times. "Fascinating, marvelous, moving and forceful." - Associated Press.* [2W]

❑ **THE YOUNG MAN FROM ATLANTA Winner of the 1995 Pulitzer Prize. by Horton Foote.** An older couple attempts to recover from the suicide death of their only son, but the menacing truth of why he died, and what a certain Young Man from Atlanta had to do with it, keeps them from the peace they so desperately need. *"Foote ladles on character and period nuances with a density unparalleled in any living playwright." - NY Newsday.* [5M, 4W]

❑ **SIMPATICO by Sam Shepard.** Years ago, two men organized a horse racing scam. Now, years later, the plot backfires against the ringleader when his partner decides to come out of hiding. *"Mr. Shepard writing at his distinctive, savage best." - New York Times.* [3M, 3W]

❑ **MOONLIGHT by Harold Pinter.** The love-hate relationship between a dying man and his family is the subject of Harold Pinter's first full-length play since *Betrayal*. *"Pinter works the language as a master pianist works the keyboard." - New York Post.* [4M, 2W, 1G]

❑ **SYLVIA by A.R. Gurney.** This romantic comedy, the funniest to come along in years, tells the story of a twenty-two year old marriage on the rocks, and of Sylvia, the dog who turns it all around. *"A delicious and dizzy new comedy." - New York Times. "FETCHING! I hope it runs longer than Cats!" - New York Daily News.* [2M, 2W]